KID
ME
NOT

KID ME NOT

An anthology by

child-free women of the '60s
now in their 60s

Edited by Aralyn Hughes

Publisher's Note

Copyright © 2014 by Aralyn Hughes
Original cover art by Aralyn Hughes
Cover design by Karen Kreps, Mary-Ellen Campbell

ISBN-13: 978-1-938749-10-0

ISBN-10: 1938749103

Dedicated to
Planned Parenthood of Texas

A portion of the royalties from the sale of this book will be donated in appreciation of its unwavering efforts on behalf of women's health and family planning despite enormous challenges.

Contents

Foreword

QUESTION OF THE DAY:
Have you ever regretted not having children?

A dear soul on (my) Facebook page asked me this the other day, and I thought I'd make the answer public. The simple answer, blessedly, is: No.

The longer answer is that I have come to believe there are three sorts of women, when it comes to questions of maternity. There are women who are born to be mothers, women who are born to be aunties, and women who should not be allowed within ten feet of a child. It can be a tragic situation (either personally, for a family, or for the community at large) when a woman ends up in the wrong category, based on her true nature. Women who long for children but cannot have babies suffer enormously, as we know. But children who are born to inadequate or unprepared mothers also suffer enormously (and their mothers suffer, too—trapped in a responsibility that they can neither meet or enjoy).

Those of us who are natural-born aunties are luckier. We love children, we enjoy children, but we know in our deepest marrow that we are not supposed to have children of our own. And that is absolutely fine, for not every woman in history needs to be a mother. Now, listen—if you put a baby in front of me, rest assured: that baby is gonna get cuddled, spoiled and adored. But even as I'm loving on that beautiful infant, I know in my heart: This is not my destiny. It never was. And there is a curious rush of joy that I feel, knowing this to be true—for it is every bit as important in life to understand who you AREN'T, as to understand who you ARE. Me, I'm just not a mom. I create in other ways. Having reached a contented and productive middle age, I can say without a blink of hesitation that I wouldn't trade my choices with anyone's.

Elizabeth Gilbert
Author of *Eat, Pray, Love*

Introduction

"No woman can call herself free who does not own and control her body. No woman can call herself free until she can choose consciously whether she will or will not be a mother."

Margaret Sanger 1879 – 1966

In the 1960s women saw the advent of the birth control pill, making theirs the first generation to have reliable options when considering whether or not to become mothers. Availability of The Pill provided women and their partners a sexual freedom never before seen in society. Their lives were further touched by social upheaval over the Vietnam War, the military draft, the struggle for civil rights and rapidly changing attitudes toward the use of drugs.

This collection of essays, written by women of the Baby Boomer generation, is not a soapbox, but it is decidedly more than a Tweet. It offers glimpses into how fifteen women were affected by a radically shifting paradigm, and how coming of age during a tumultuous decade influenced their decisions, resulting in the lives they live today.

Kid Me Not does not pass judgment on any woman's choice. It is simply the outcome of my asking women who came of age in the sixties, all of us now in our sixties, to step forward and share their personal experiences—specifically those which led them, either by choice or default, to live their lives child free.

Most of us are not writers by profession. We drafted our pieces and formed small groups, giving one another, over a period of several months, encouragement and constructive feedback. I am proud that these women, my friends, found the courage to write honest, straightforward accounts of how they chose to shape their lives, circumnavigating the established path to motherhood, so long expected of women.

I liken us to pioneer women who took a break from our individual journeys, to circle the wagons and sit around a campfire telling our stories. We have listened to each one carefully, mindful of the rich thread of history that runs through every life.

Because I am an artist whose work often involves storytelling, I feel compelled to encourage the same in others. I urge you to take time to listen, really listen, to women of all ages when they speak of their journeys through life. And don't be afraid to share your own.

I invite you to join me and my friends as we share stories. Come closer, sit by our fire. Listen.

Aralyn Hughes, *Editor*

I shall be telling this with a sigh
Somewhere ages and ages hence:
Two roads diverged in a wood, and I—
I took the one less traveled by,
And that has made all the difference.

Robert Frost
The Road Not Taken

~ *It Happened in... 1960* ~

Nixon-Kennedy debate: 70 million viewers
Kennedy: first Catholic US president
Khrushchev orders construction of Berlin Wall
USSR shoots down U2 spy plane
OPEC is formed
US announces it will send 3,500 troops to Vietnam
Elvis leaves the Army
Nazi Adolph Eichmann captured in Argentina
Cassius Clay: Gold medal, Rome Olympics
UK lifts 32-year ban on "Lady Chatterley's Lover"
Playboy Club opens in Chicago
Xerox: first copying machine
First US telephone answering machine
First pacemaker, US
Aluminum cans introduced

TV: *Gunsmoke; Have Gun Will Travel; Perry Mason;*
77 Sunset Strip; Father Knows Best; Ed Sullivan Show

TV debuts: *The Flintstones; Andy Griffith Show*

Canceled: *Howdy Doody*

Films: *Psycho; Where the Boys Are; Exodus; Ocean's Eleven;*
Please Don't Eat the Daisies

Tunes: *I'm Sorry; Cathy's Clown; Teen Angel;*
Itsy Bitsy Teeny Weeny Yellow Polka Dot Bikini;
A Summer Place; Are You Lonesome Tonight; The Twist

~ 1961 ~

Eisenhower warns against 'military industrial complex'
Peace Corp established
JFK asks for $531 million to put a man on the moon
Castro declares Cuba is Communist
Bay of Pigs
USSR detonates hydrogen bomb: largest explosion in history
Kennedy advises US: Build bomb shelters (see above)
Outlawed: *Segregation on trains in the South*
First disposable diapers
First electric toothbrush
Hot new typewriter: IBM Selectric
Alan Shepard: first American in space
TWA: first in-flight movie
Julia Child: "Mastering the Art of French Cooking"
New: *Fritos*
Barbie gets a boyfriend: Ken
New: *The Pendletones (Later: The Beach Boys)*

Canceled: *I Love Lucy*

Film: *Breakfast at Tiffany's*
Tunes: *Runaround Sue; Will You Love Me Tomorrow; Stand By Me; Crying; Moon River; Take Good Care of My Baby; Dedicated to the One I Love*

Born: *Barack Obama; Princess Diana; Meg Ryan; George Clooney; Melissa Ethridge*
Death: *Ernest Hemingway, suicide*

COLORING OUTSIDE THE LINES

by Aralyn Hughes

I was 38 and childless when a friend, whose husband worked overseas for months at a time, asked me to be her birthing coach. I was honored to accept, and also thrilled. I'd decided many years earlier not to have children. The chance to participate actively in a birth was a gift. As the months went by, working with her, I became almost as excited about the baby as she was.

When it was time, we rushed to the hospital. Watching my friend as she suffered through excruciating pain, I felt helpless. Finally, the big moment came. First, the crowning of the head, then the episiotomy, and before I knew it, out that baby came. Soon my friend was home, a new mother.

Having seen her endure nine months of discomfort during pregnancy and the horrendous pain of childbirth, I could hardly believe my ears when she told me she wanted to have a second child. Now a seasoned pro, I was thrilled to help her again. And together we went through it all once more. As her children grew from infants in cribs to toddlers in nursery school, I picked them up from school, helped with birthday parties, and babysat, to give my friend much-needed afternoon breaks.

One day she invited me to a workshop, at which the leaders gave us an exercise where we were to choose five people from the group to take aboard a spaceship to start a new civilization. Without hesitation I put her name on my list. She, however, did not put mine on hers. I was shocked. When I asked why, she said, "Because you don't have children and don't want to have children." My feelings were hurt beyond measure. Did she think I had no value because I chose to be childless? Was I completely useless to society in her eyes?

After the workshop she became distant and gradually terminated our friendship. When I asked why, she told me, "I have children now. I have nothing in common with you." I remember replying, "After all I've done for you?" I realize I was unaware of the round-the-clock demands of motherhood. Maybe she'd become so overwhelmed by it she'd been forced to decide who she could afford to keep in her life and who she couldn't. Regardless, I had become dispensable. Again and again I would see this pattern; my friends who had children slowly but surely disappeared from my life. Often they would drop a frustrating comment or two about my decision to not have children. I heard similar comments from steadier friends as well as from family members. Most of the people I knew seemed unable to fathom such a departure from the norm. Here are the comments I heard most often.

1. *"You must have had a bad childhood."*

Until the year my mother died, she called me on my birthday to tell me this story: "I wasn't sure I wanted another child after your brother was born. He was a big baby—nine pounds. I didn't know if I could go through that again. But after my own mother died, I started longing for another child, this time a girl. Several months into the pregnancy with you, they took an x-ray—they did that back then—and the doctor told me the baby had such big hands and feet it was probably going to be another boy. I tried to hide my disappointment.

"When I went into labor, that childbirth was every bit as difficult as the first one. But then I heard, 'It's a girl! Nine pounds, all toes and fingers.' I looked to the heavens and said, "Thank you. I will never ask for anything else. I have my bundle of joy."

I never tired of hearing it. My parents grew up in the Depression and lived through the Dust Bowl in Oklahoma where I was born. Those hard times gave my parents perspective. Anything good that happened was a blessing; anything bad could be managed. My mother and father lived to be 94 and 95, respectively.

I wasn't the perfect child, but they were very nearly the perfect parents. They rolled with punches and knew how to balance boundaries and independence, expectations and creativity. My relationship with my mom was so connected and unconditional I found it almost daunting as I grew older. I worried I might be unable to recreate such a bond. Further, she'd given over her whole life to me. She was the Girl Scout leader, the Bible school superintendent, the aide to the children's choir at church, the gifted seamstress who made cheerleading outfits and prom dresses, and the talented and hard-working cook who made luscious coconut cream pies and whose fried chicken and gravy were legendary.

What if a child of mine just couldn't connect with me? Or worse, what if being a mother didn't bring me the joy it clearly brought my mom? Doubts filled my head when I imagined myself with children. If I chose that life, how would I ever get anything else done? I wanted to do things. I wanted to travel. I wanted to create art. Could I give my entire life to a child as my mother had? And, more importantly, should I? Would it be the right decision for me? Could I be happy as a parent as she so clearly was? Was that the right lifestyle for me? I knew even then it wasn't. I felt it in my gut. I just knew I would have to walk a different path.

2. *"You would have been a great mother."*

Like most girls, I grew up assuming I would be a wife, mother, and homemaker, believing that "the hand that rocked the cradle ruled the nation." In high school, I was President of the Future Homemakers of America and in college I even went so far as to get a Bachelor's of Science degree in Home Economics.

But babysitting in my teens brought out in me a degree of frustration and anger so extreme it shocked me—I wanted to toss those kids over the balcony.

With tears streaming down my face, I called my mother, who was just down the street. She came immediately and took over, utterly amazing me by how easy and natural it was for her to supervise kids.

"It's different when they're your own," she said, trying to console me. As an awkward teenager with no role models other than the conventional ones, I saw no alternative but to follow in her footsteps lest, God forbid, I should grow up to be an old maid. Yet as an adult, my experiences as aunt to my brother's three children, a junior high teacher, and a witness to the dubious behavior of most of my friends' children, made me grateful for my freedom. I found little appealing in the prospect of making an 18-year commitment, as they had, to a life I regarded as tumultuous.

Though I may not have been cut out to be a mother, I think I would've been a good dad. My dad left the house for work each morning, made the family's money, and managed all the financial decisions. He was involved in politics and community service. He taught me how to ride my bike and how to play fair with others in games. He guided me through my fear of spiders, showed me how to safely handle fireworks, and taught me my first lessons in how things work in the universe. He was the head of the house except when it came to homemaking and parenting. In those areas, Mom was in charge.

Dad was solid and made me feel safe, but he was not the one I went to when I was upset. If I was heartbroken, crying over not getting some award at school or other perceived teenage tragedy, he would walk into the room and say, "Next week you won't even remember this. In the whole scheme of things it won't even register." Then Mom would yell from the kitchen, "Paul, she doesn't want to hear that right now!"

The truth is I was always more like my dad than my mom. But nobody ever thought to say, "You'd make a great dad."

3. *"Childbirth isn't all that bad."*

On Memorial Day when I was growing up in Oklahoma, we would place plastic wreaths on the gravesites of relatives in the country cemeteries. When I was old enough to read the dates on the tombstones I wondered why some of the females had died so young. I was hardly comforted when I overheard grownups say, "Bless her heart, she died in childbirth." Although giving birth is a much safer proposition today, no one's ever convinced me it's a sure thing.

The severe cramps I suffered from puberty onward added to my anxieties around childbirth. I questioned the wisdom of spending half my adult life suffering through my periods just to be able to have children I was less and less sure I even wanted. During my cheer-leading days, my periods were almost unbearable. I suffered horrendous hot and cold flashes and sometimes passed blood clots the size of olives. It was embarrassing and humiliating having to leave school, pale and in pain.

The bloating, the hot flashes, the bad moods were so extreme every month that I would actually consider suicide. Some doctors had the gall to tell my mother it was all in my head. As an adult, my cramps were still so bad I talked to doctors about having my tubes tied. Invariably, they did all they could to dissuade me, assuring me I would one day change my mind about having a baby. They were wrong. At age 48, I had a hysterectomy. If I could go back in time, knowing what I know now, I would have had the procedure when I was twelve.

4. "When are we going to hear the pitter patter of little feet?"

In 1968, at age 21, I married a young military man. Immediately my parents and friends began asking when I was going to start a family, how many children I planned to have. And they wanted assurances I'd be a stay-at-home mom.

My own community and society at large, whether overtly or subtly, maintained that Virginity, Marriage, and Motherhood (the holy trinity) represented the surest route to Heaven on Earth any woman could take. I was a junior in college when the university's health center began offering birth control for married or engaged students. Flashing my diamond engagement ring as proof I qualified, I braced myself for that first terrifying pelvic exam. Having survived it, I got a prescription for birth control pills. In those days The Pill was so strong, it made me sick. During a fitting for my wedding dress, I almost threw up all over it.

On my honeymoon night, a shy and embarrassed virgin, I tried to figure out where my husband's arms and legs, as well as my own, were supposed to go. Sylvia Plath's descriptive line from The Bell Jar, comparing a penis to "turkey necks and turkey gizzards" popped to mind. I silently asked myself, "For this I waited?" More than anything, I wanted to call my mother to come over and sort it all out for me.

As the wife of a naval officer who was either depressed or out to sea, marriage left me feeling strangely alone. I stood by watching as the other military wives had children, noticing that they, too, were alone, stranded far from their families. One of these military wives confided in me her belief that men were only good for bringing home money, adding that when it came to raising children they were "as useless as tits on a boar hog."

I came to know the wife of my husband's commanding officer. She and I played canasta and bridge and often shared Saturday night dinners when our husbands were out to sea. One day, I asked her point-blank to tell me the truth: what is it like to have children? She said, "I love my children, would lie on the tracks in front of an oncoming train to protect them. But if I were you, I wouldn't do it. Go have fun, see the world; be creative, independent, and free. You can have an ex-husband, an ex-job and an ex-hometown, but children are forever."

5. *"Children make your marriage stronger."*

It seemed that everyone, except for my military-wife friend who'd bluntly told the truth as she saw it, had a vested interest in my having children. Again and again my husband and family would press me on it. Friends assured me that children would strengthen my marriage. But I was having serious doubts about the marriage and thought it better to hold off until we got it in better order.

We never did. For me marriage just wasn't what it was cracked up to be. It felt like I'd been given a snow job, sold a bill of goods as to the joys awaiting me in the trinity of Virginity, Marriage, and Children. After nine years, and with my continuing to say no to our having a baby, my husband filed for divorce. I was thankful there were no children to connect the two of us forever. Over time, I saw that it was not in my nature to live a traditional life. I chose to be neither monogamous, nor to settle down. Just as some women thrive on the joys and challenges of motherhood with a single mate, the course that felt most natural, and made me happiest, was to have an adventurous sex life with multiple partners. I accepted this fact, and lived it.

6. *"Who will take care of you in your golden years?"*

An unmarried male friend with whom I used to go white water rafting recently died in his sleep. His body was not discovered for six days. The news made me realize the same thing could happen to me.

When I was absolutely certain I would remain childless, I began saving money like a mad woman, bought long-term health insurance, and wrote a will outlining my wishes after my death. I named one friend to be responsible for the decision to pull the plug and another as her back up. I told them both I did not want to be kept alive if it was clear I could no longer have any fun or be any fun. I joked that if it gets to the point where I'm not telling stories or wanting to dance, that is the time to set me adrift. I think friends could do this more easily than my older brother who lives far away and is traditionally religious.

I never regarded children as some kind of insurance policy for one's golden years. My parents flatly refused to move in with me or even move to my city when they got older, and if I had a child I would have followed their example. I took care of my parents when they were dying because I wanted to, not out of a sense of obligation. They told me, "It would not make us happy to know you missed a single beat in your life, sacrificed anything for us, or mourned when we are gone. We have had a wonderful life, two wonderful kids, and a great community. There is nothing more that we could ask for, and we're grateful and ready to go when the time comes." I teared up when Mom said, "I can't live forever, honey." Then she teared up as she told me, "It's going to be so hard to leave you."

In lieu of having children to depend on, through the years I've forged a community of many close, mostly single friends who take care of one another. Recently one of us was diagnosed with throat cancer. After her surgery, which included a tracheotomy and a feeding tube, several of us created a schedule in six-hour shifts so that one of us would always be with her. We maintained this support from the time she entered the hospital until she stabilized at home months later.

So, what is family? How is it best defined? Must you be related by blood? If that's true, then how does marriage make a family of the husband and wife? Could a group of dear friends who are witness to each others lives, who grow old together and pledge to support one another in sickness and in health, till death do they part, be anything less?

7. "You're selfish."

I was the administrator/director of the first abortion clinic in Austin, Texas. No woman who ever came to us wanted to be there. So often their situations were the result of their having been trained to deny their sexuality, leaving them ill-prepared in matters of birth control when their natural instincts took over. In my clinic, I assisted Catholic women, Asian women, rich women, Ph.D. students, ministers' wives, and women from smaller towns nearby. Teenagers, in most cases, came alone. Men were almost as rare as parents.

The relief I saw in the eyes of women leaving the clinic made that job the most gratifying I ever had. They were so grateful for our kindness and support and lack of judgment. It was easy for me to provide compassion, empathy, respect, support, and education to these women. The most painful to see were the many incest victims, ten to fifteen years old. I never got used to that, and could hardly believe how frequently it happened. If I'd been raising children, would I have had the energy to serve those women with the attention and care they needed? Was that a selfish choice on my part?

Parents who did come to the clinic could be irrational, angry, and unstable. The result of years of frustration with their children, as well as themselves, played out in horrific scenes. Some of those parents abandoned their children. Over my years there, I took into my home three different troubled teens with the hope of providing a safe space for them to recover before they made their next move.

Although I enjoyed them, I found extended contact with kids to be drain-ing. I did not understand then, nor do I now, how parents maintain themselves under such constant demands. I admire them for it; I also admire birds for flying, but I'm in no hurry to jump off a roof and flap my wings.

8. "You will regret not having children."

One day the unthinkable happened. Although I'd taken every precaution, I—the woman who'd decided over and over against having children, who taught others about birth control—became pregnant herself. I was healthy and had a decent partner and stable finances. But as I once again weighed the option of having a child, I knew in my heart it would be the wrong choice.

I felt like a failure and was furious with myself, as well as plenty embarrassed to be a patient at my own clinic. But accidents happen. They always will, as I'd seen over and over. When I chose abortion, I put the issue to bed finally and permanently. I would never have children in this lifetime, and I would never marry again. Those decisions went hand in hand.

I have wondered on occasion what a child of mine might look like or be like. How I would have felt driving my kids to school every day in the Suburban, trying to manage their temper tantrums in the grocery store, rocking and singing them to sleep in the middle of the night when they were sick with a fever. I wonder how hard I would have been on myself for not being the perfect mom. Very hard, I suspect.

I'm a creative person, so it is not lost on me that I missed out on the ultimate creation—birthing a child. I won't deny it. My mother never said a word, but I doubt she fully understood the choice I made. I'd like to think she secretly admired me, supported the nontraditional path I took, and wondered at times what it would have been like for her to live my life of independence and sexual freedom. Our finite lives force these choices on us, and for every step we choose, there is a step we didn't choose. Wherever our choices take us, we're left wondering about the road not taken.

My decision to live as I have did not make my life perfect nor did it offer me sheer bliss. I'm sure that's true for all women, with or without children. Nothing is perfect, but I am content with what is. I must admit the road I've taken has been pretty darn interesting and fun. More importantly, even with the disappointments and hardships that came, I've never regretted having chosen to walk down it.

9. *"Don't you want to leave your genes behind, your legacy?"*

My husband felt a strong need to leave his genes behind. This is probably instinctive; perhaps even a species-directive, for many people. Having a child can serve as a buffer to the fact that your life really is finite. There's that son or daughter, a living person coded with half your genetic material, who will carry on. For me, such concerns were never important. I think much of this is simply due to my makeup. But there was also a series of writers who influenced me.

The first was Paul Ehrlich, who, in his 1968 book, The Population Bomb, warned how overpopulation was going to dramatically affect the world of the future. Next, I read Rachel Carson's Silent Spring, in which she detailed the many ways we are destroying the environment. Such grim predictions made me feel less compelled to continue my bloodline. Then Charles A. Reich, in The Greening of America, opened my mind to the counterculture and alternate lifestyles. That was when I realized I did not have to follow an expected, traditional path.

But if I wasn't driven to birthing babies, I discovered I was driven to birthing creative projects as my legacy to leave. I regret being dismissive of mothers and fathers who wanted to leave behind something of themselves by having a child. The creative impulse, whether it's expressed in the raising of a child, the building of a bridge, or in artistic endeavors, is surely one of life's primal forces driving us all.

Along with my many paintings, my current art projects focus on telling my life's story through stage performances, in a documentary movie, and, most recently, in this book.

Without having children to pass along my story, I feel the need to speak for myself. It's just as well; I'm afraid a child of mine might get it wrong or leave out the good parts.

Remember the woman who did not choose me to go on her spaceship? After her children were grown, some twenty-seven years later, we spoke and she raised the idea of renewing our friendship. She said that despite our not being as close as we once were, she still considered me a friend, someone she could rely on. I had to tell her the truth. Since she hadn't been there for me then, I wasn't sure I could be there for her now. Really, I wasn't sure I trusted that she'd appreciate my friendship enough not to reject me yet again. Of course, time had lessened my pain, but I just wasn't willing to take the chance.

If, however, I could return to that day when I was asked to select five people to begin a new civilization, this time I would be more practical. I wouldn't hesitate to choose for my spaceship women who wanted to bring children into our brave new world—mothers. But because I better understand how very consuming the job of mothering is, I'd feel the need to tag along to assure that creativity and the arts were given their proper place, as they are in all great cultures. I can easily see myself serving as both a birthing coach and as Director of the Arts, continuing to do what I do best: coloring outside the lines.

Aralyn's life is focused on creativity, art and story. Through her work as a visual and performance artist, she has learned that when she risks being seen, making herself vulnerable out there on the skinny branches, those experiences bring her the most joy.

NORMA INMAN

AN OLD SOUL

by Norma Inman

Nearly half a century has not erased the terror I felt on learning I was pregnant. Though the birth control pill was available in the early 1960s, nice girls who were single did not take them because nice girls had no need for them since "nice" was synonymous with "virgin." Passing myself off as a nice girl, I could hardly take advantage of this product before I was married. To obtain a prescription required a visit to our family doctor. He would ask embarrassing questions and probably inform my mother, who surely would subject me to endless harangues about my moral decay and tell me I would never find anyone willing to marry me.

I never considered myself "easy," in the parlance of the early '60s, but I did think it unfair that boys were allowed to sow their seeds indiscriminately while girls were expected to subvert sexual desires until their wedding nights. I still wonder how many of my friends actually succeeded in doing that. I certainly did not. I lost my virginity to my high school "steady" and consider it no small miracle I did not become pregnant until I was nineteen. My periods were always irregular, and I would not be surprised if on more than one occasion I was pregnant and miscarried.

There is no way to explain to young women today the stigma of unwed pregnancy in the early 1960s. It must be remembered that the Sexual Revolution did not occur until late in the '60s when the pill became more easily obtainable. Until that time, the most common way of dealing with an out-of-wedlock pregnancy was to marry. This was the solution for a friend who found herself pregnant at sixteen. As was routinely done in these cases, the marriage was passed off as having secretly occurred several months before its announcement. Even with this façade, the expectant mother was forced to transfer to another high school. Heaven forbid the expectant father, a football star, transfer and break the school's winning streak.

Another pregnant friend was sent away under the guise of helping an elderly relative; the child was given up for adoption. There were rumors that another girl's baby brother was actually her child. These were the pretenses of respectability erected around such events in those times.

R.C., the father of my child, and I were madly in love but neither of us wanted a child. We were putting ourselves through college by working part-time jobs and living on a shoestring. We agreed the only feasible solution was an abortion. Finding an abortionist in 1964 was no easy feat—abortion was illegal. As we began asking friends, who allegedly had experience in such matters, the standard response was "go to Mexico," though no one could tell us how to locate a doctor once we were there. I considered self-aborting by throwing myself down the stairs at my boarding house, falling off a horse, or using knitting needles to pry the fetus from my uterus, but I lacked the nerve to pursue those methods.

Time was running out for an abortion in the first trimester. R.C. and I decided to marry and continue our search for an abortionist. We dropped out of school and purchased a wedding license and rings. Without us knowing, the school notified our parents we had withdrawn. One morning, R.C. awoke to a pounding on his door and his father's voice calling his name. When he opened the door, he was confronted by his father and uncle demanding to know why he had dropped out of school. They insisted he return home with them. A few days later I received a letter from him telling me he had decided it was not in our best interest to marry. Shortly thereafter he left the state.

Reading his letter I was bewildered, heartbroken, and distraught that this man whom I loved with the kind of passion found only in youth could so easily abandon me and abuse my trust. He had promised me that we would get through this crisis together. Now he was gone, and suddenly the pregnancy was my problem. I was devastated. I had no choice but to go home.

It often occurred to me that men were the lucky ones when it came to sex and children. They could indulge themselves with absolutely no fear of pregnancy or harm to their reputation. There were several boys who were rumored to have fathered children and they suffered no ill effects whatsoever. If anything, it gave them a bad-boy aura.

As I watched my friends marry, have children, and divorce, the women usually retained custody of the children while the man might, or might not, pay adequate child support and take an active role in the lives of his children. Men quickly returned to a relatively unfettered bachelor lifestyle while the women were forced to juggle home, children, and usually a job with never enough time or money. I envied men their freedom of obligation when it came to children and their ability to continue their lives relatively child-free after a divorce while continuing to pursue their education, goals, and dreams.

My parents had reared me to believe that there were no limitations on my abilities and that I could accomplish whatever I set my mind to. As a young girl, I read voraciously, usually books about women: Marie Curie, Florence Nightingale, Annie Oakley, Sacagawea, Joan of Arc, Cleopatra, Pollyanna, Nancy Drew, Queen Elizabeth I, and Queen Victoria. All these stories inspired me and created a spirit of independence that made me long to follow the road less traveled. For me, that road did not have children on it.

But now I was pregnant and it seemed my only option was to go through with the pregnancy and place the child for adoption. My mother, possessing a sixth sense that I inherited, had surmised the reason behind my return home. When she found me retching into the toilet one morning, I confirmed her suspicions. She replied, "We'll have to find an abortionist." Was I shocked or surprised by this? Not at all. Throughout my youth, my mother often spoke of abortion as an acceptable end to an unwanted pregnancy. After she died I learned that she sought an abortion for one of her pregnancies. Because it was too far advanced, the doctor refused.

My mother was many things: highly intelligent, vindictive, controlling, witty, a pathological liar, manipulative, sly, and very resourceful. She had contacts, and it was through one of them, a hospital administrator, that she found a local doctor who performed abortions. The next obstacle was the cost, $600—more than $4,000 in today's dollars. Fortunately, my brother had several thousand dollars saved and I was able to borrow the money from him under some ruse I no longer remember. My abortion was performed November 17, 1964, in the doctor's unmarked office without benefit of pain killers or anesthetic. The pain was excruciating. Lying on the table fully clothed, except for my panties, in the event a quick exit was required, I thought the procedure would never end. The only ill effects I suffered were emotional. It was R.C., not my mother, I wanted by my side sharing this emotional time with me.

Being pregnant made me understand for the first time the desire for a child. I felt protectiveness and a bond with the child I carried ever so briefly that confirmed I had a maternal instinct. For many years after the abortion, I would think of the child who might have been and how old it would be. To this day, very few people know about the abortion; it was not something I discussed, even with my closest friends. There were no support groups for women who had had abortions, so I bore my grief alone and in silence. My mother and I never discussed the abortion except after, when she was driving me home. She told me I had done the right thing, and now I needed to get on with my life and forget about R.C. Getting on with my life was easy; I became a flight attendant based in New York City. Forgetting R.C. was not.

"Nearly half a century has not erased the terror I felt on learning I was pregnant."

Six months after my abortion I was at a party when I felt a hand on my waist. I turned to see whose it was and couldn't believe my eyes. We hadn't seen one another, much less spoken, in nine months, but as R.C. embraced me, holding me so tight I could hardly breathe, I realized he hadn't wanted us to break up any more than I had. We needed to talk, to reconnect away from the curious eyes of our friends. Once we were alone I could barely contain my fury as he told me the awful truth of why he'd left me.

True to form, my meddling mother had set into motion the events that led to R.C.'s abandoning me. As soon as she was notified I'd dropped out of college, she suspected I must be pregnant and contemplating marrying R. C. When she called his parents and learned that he also had dropped out, she did what any good mother would do: she lied. The marriage must be stopped for R.C.'s own good. Why? Because, my mother told them, I was mentally unstable.

R.C. was all of twenty years old. He listened to his parents. He knew he was being lied to, but he felt obligated to appease them, to give in to their demands. So he broke up with me and left town. Listening to him tell me of my mother's deceitfulness, I was stunned. But I knew the woman and what she was capable of. I didn't doubt a word of the sorry tale R.C. told me that night.

R.C. and I wed six months later, on the day he was to take his physical to be drafted and most likely sent to Vietnam. During that first year I tried to talk with him about the desperation I'd felt when he left me, how much easier it would have been for me emotionally if he'd been there when I had the abortion. He didn't want to discuss it. That was in the past; what mattered now was that we were together and happy.

We were married for twelve years. I worked as a secretary while he completed his degree in electrical engineering, and then he supported me for my undergraduate and graduate degrees in political science. Like my parents, he pushed me to excel and do things I did not think myself capable of, such as going to graduate school and pursuing a career as a political consultant.

I left him after taking a position as a lobbyist for the Equal Rights Amendment. The job required I relocate to the state capital. We thought we would be able to maintain a long-distance marriage, but soon found our schedules seldom overlapped. Each of us was devoting all of our energies to succeeding in our respective careers and that left little energy or time for our marriage. When I told him I was leaving, he began to weep and said, "You're getting even for the abortion, aren't you?" It was the first, and last, indication he ever gave that he had some understanding of the emotional pain I'd suffered over the abortion.

Another factor in my decision not to have children was my mother's answer when, in my early teens, I asked her what it was like to have a baby. How much pain was involved? Her reply was that the pain was similar to what I went through with monthly cramps only worse. No way am I putting myself through that, I thought, since my monthly cramping was so severe I often vomited or passed out.

While working on a paper on abortion in graduate school, I came across research showing that those women who do not want children are as fervent in their desire as are women who want a child. I know that is true of me. When I was in my twenties and thirties, people would ask when I planned to start a family. When I answered that a family was not in my plans they would say, "You'll change your mind." Over time I learned not to argue. I knew I was committed to my decision.

When I was thirty-two, I had my tubes tied. When I was forty-four, I had a hysterectomy. Finally, I was free from the monthly pain I had endured since my first period.

Just as memorable as my abortion was the day I heard the Supreme Court's decision in Roe v. Wade. I broke down and sobbed uncontrollably as the news was announced on the radio. All I could think was, Thank God! Now other women can be spared the torment and pain I went through in 1964.

I hold in high esteem my friends who have children. They possess a self-lessness, fortitude, and patience that I lack. I've never regretted my decision to be childless because it allowed me to live the life I wanted, one that never would have been possible with children. I think of my friends' children and the college students I teach as my surrogate children. In many ways, I have the relationships with them that I envied in so many men. I am able to pick and choose when and how I interact with them and then leave and enjoy my independence. I can be their Auntie Mame, bestowing gifts, time, and attention on my own schedule.

A friend once told me that the Chinese believe those who choose not to have children are old souls who see no need to procreate since that was accomplished in their other lives. Perhaps that explains why I have no regrets, remorse, or guilt over my decision.

Norma and her husband of thirty years live on a ranch in the Texas Hill Country. She is on retainer with an oil and gas exploration company, teaches political science courses and sells antiques and vintage clothing.

"By and large, mothers and housewives are the only workers who do not have regular time off. They are the great vacationless class."

Anne Morrow Lindbergh

~ 1962 ~

Av cost of new home: $12,500

Av yearly income: $5,956

Harvard tuition: $1,500/yr

Dozen eggs: 32 cents

Telstar relays first live trans-Atlantic television signal

Walter Cronkite: CBS Evening News

Johnny Carson: The Tonight Show

Cuban Missile Crisis

Wal-Mart opens, Bentonville, AR

Ranger IV: First US rocket lands on the moon

John Glenn: First American to orbit Earth

James Meredith enters U of MS; 500 U.S. Marshals sent

First Bond film: Dr. No

Let's Dance! The Twist; Mashed Potatoes; Pony

Debut*: Pantyhose (Bye-bye, garter belts!)*

First silicone breast implants, Houston

Unveiled*: Campbell's Soup Can, Andy Warhol*

Decca turns down record deal w/ Beatles

Beatles first single: Love Me Do

TV*: Beverly Hillbillies; Candid Camera; What's My Line?*

Films*: Days of Wine & Roses; To Kill a Mockingbird; Lolita;
Whatever Happened to Baby Jane?*

Tunes*: Big Girls Don't Cry; Al di La; Peppermint Twist;
Duke of Earl; The Lion Sleeps Tonight; Johnny Angel; Breaking
Up Is Hard to Do; Soldier Boy; Sherry; Telstar*

Born*: Sheryl Crow; Jody Foster; Joan Cusack; Garth Brooks;
Tom Cruise; Tammy Baldwin; Jackie-Joyner Kersee; Bon-Jovi;
Felicity Huffman; Naomi Wolf*

Death*: Marilyn Monroe, ruled suicide*

BIOLOGY

by Kathleen Juhl

I didn't know I was a lesbian. What I did know was that I didn't want to have kids.

The '60s were a blur. I was in high school and had these weird feelings for my gym teachers, but had no idea what they meant. It was Iowa. I was naïve. I didn't know what a lesbian was! But I didn't date boys until I met Rob.

And after college, in 1976, I married him knowing I didn't love him and with this feeling in my gut that I just might get trapped. So I refused to change my last name. And I told Rob I didn't want kids. And he said that was okay by him. Perfect! Marrying him— something you did in Iowa in the 1970s—meant I wouldn't have to escape Iowa alone, and I wouldn't have to have kids.

Why no kids? I wanted to go to graduate school, wanted a career. Had no biological urge to put a life into my belly. And I flat-out didn't like kids. Never had. They made me antsy and anxious and impatient. Too much baby sitting? I don't know…I just didn't like 'em!

After Rob and I had slogged along for three years, he suddenly changed his mind. Started talking about babies. I'll take care of them, he said. But I don't want a kid, I said.

And then I met a woman. A lesbian. I was fascinated. Attracted. So I dumped Rob and got outta Dodge. Moved in with Ann, who had two kids! Good god! I don't know what I was doing! I didn't love her, I was just flattered. I was twenty-five.

She was thirty-one and thought I was gorgeous. Mostly, though, she wasn't Rob.

She said, "Love me, love my kids," and I said, "Sure!" What was I thinking?! Did I have a hidden desire to fulfill my culturally constructed female role in the world? Did I feel guilty for not having children, for not liking children? I honestly don't know.

But here they were, two kids. Girls. Five and eight. The little one was sweet and smart and fun. The other was sullen, a real problem child. She couldn't relate to me. I couldn't relate to her. I was just not good with her. And I was certainly not good with her mother. We fought all the time. Dysfunction. Bad vibes all around, and it hurt the girls.

But I stayed and finished two masters degrees, got a teaching job in Texas, navigated a rocky road to a Ph.D., tried to be a partner and parent—a complicated juggling act. I have no idea how I survived. But through it all, more and more, I knew I'd been right. Should've trusted my instincts: I had no business parenting kids.

"I didn't know I was a lesbian. What I did know was I didn't want kids."

The girls grew up wild, both of them. The sweet one became rebellious; the sullen one stayed sullen. I blamed myself. They both got pregnant, got married. Neither went to college despite my begging that they at least check it out. If I was going to raise kids, was it too much to hope they'd be a little bit like me? I was desperate about it. But it didn't pan out. I was frustrated and sad, especially about the sweet and smart kid.

Oh, how I had hoped that the sweet, smart kid would go to college, have a career, become someone for me to talk to, to relate to. No dice.

And yet, I stayed. I stayed for thirty long, miserable years. And all the while, I knew I didn't belong in that scene. I told myself I was staying for the kids…and the five grandkids that later came along. I tried, truly I did. I tried to love my partner and I tried to love those kids, all of them. I tried. But I failed. I'd never wanted kids. Period.

I wanted those graduate degrees and that career.

The job was teaching theatre at a small private college where, in the '80s and '90s, it was not cool to be a lesbian. But if I talked about my kids and grandkids, I could be incognito. If I talked about the kids and the grandkids, no one would suspect I was a lesbian and deny me tenure. The kids! They were good for something! They were my cover. But my ethics and my conscience? Nowhere to be found.

I loved my students, but in my private life I felt oppressed and guilty. I was surrounded and stifled and trapped by those other kids, the ones I had adopted through my promises to Ann. None of these kids and grandkids were my kids. I developed "mother guilt" anyway. I should like these kids. I should love these kids. I should stay in a bad relationship for these kids. I should sacrifice.

But I didn't want kids.

And I resented having to sacrifice for those kids. Those kids I mostly didn't like, except for the sweet one, even though she never went to college. Those kids who were not mine. Dilemmas. Confusion.

Still, I sacrificed. Personally. Hours of kid-drama. Dollars and disappointment.

Conflict and . . .

CONFESSION: It was social class.

This mother and her kids with whom I spent half my life came from a different social class. Lower middle class. Higher education and the arts were not a priority. Not even on the radar. Here I was, a theatre professor with a lot of privilege. Who was I to abandon this family? Because I was better than they were?

I told myself I had to stay, to prove I was a liberal academic who understood class privilege. I wasn't going to be a classist academic bitch. And I was miserable. I didn't want those kids—and yet, the little one, the sweet smart one... I was torn, I was confused.

Then, in the midst of all this, my only sister, my younger sister who is also a lesbian and also has a partner with two kids—two wonderful, smart kids— my little sister decided she just had to have a baby, too.

And I didn't get it.

I couldn't get it.

She had biological urges; I did not. Didn't understand 'em. Couldn't fathom why my sister wanted a baby of her own when she was surrounded by her partner's two bright, talented, amazing children.

Just did not get it.

And I hurt my sister.

I couldn't talk to her.

She couldn't talk to me.

Two lesbian sisters.

What does that mean anyway? Sisters, but in more ways than just our biological urges for and against babies, we are very different humans. And yet, it is biology. She is my sister and she was in psychic and emotional pain beyond belief over her inability, despite desperate attempts such as artificial insemination, fertilization treatments, in vitro fertilization, desperation, and obsession—to have a kid.

So I thought about obligation, duty. How I should support my sister? I tried and I failed.

I thought about our parents, who had failed us both.

When they found out that we were lesbians, they rejected us. They rejected us for eighteen years. A couple of peaceniks who couldn't deal with the reality of the progressive politics they'd professed all their lives.

My father literally went nuts. Therapy. Rehab. My mother stood by him. She loved him more than she loved her daughters. But she kept on loving my brother. My mother gave up her daughters for her husband and her son for eighteen years.

For thirty years, I stayed with a partner and kids not of my biology, whom I really did not love.

Unable to understand my sister's long painful journey toward failed biological motherhood...

Biology...

My brother has a Catholic farm-girl-wife who has eight siblings. She was desperate for a child. She thought she couldn't have a child, so she and my brother adopted a Korean baby and then got pregnant.

Biology...

I love my eighty-eight-year-old cousin more than I love my mother.

I love my new partner's brother more than I love my biological brother.

But duty calls.

Just as duty called for thirty years without the biology.

Duty called, and I answered. After an eighteen-year estrangement from my biological parents and brother, I was able to reconcile those relationships and now I am helping to care for my mother who is in a nursing home.

It seems to me that it was all symbolic biology.

"Love me, love my kids." YES! OF COURSE, YES! Ain't I a woman?

Love your parents. No matter what! That reconciliation was one more difficult and rocky road, but I did it! And it is the best thing I ever did. I really believe that. Biology—so important.

An obligation. A duty. A life commitment.

A female duty. A female life commitment.

And I chose to be with Ann.

For thirty years.

Half my life.

No biology.

And my parents? I suffered a lot of abuse in order to restore that connection with biology.

In those eighteen years, biology got swept away because I was a biological aberration. A lesbian.

Ironies. So many ironies.

I didn't want kids. Yet I walked of my own free will through a door knowing there were kids on the other side. Kids not of my biology, kids not of my class.

Thankfully, I gave birth to another life, one intellectual and professional and aesthetic and happy.

And, just as I escaped Iowa all those years ago, I escaped Ann. And I found

Sarah. Wonderful, fun, and loving Sarah, who makes me laugh, who talks with me, who treats me well and vise versa.

And that sweet smart kid I helped raise? We have a great relationship. I call her "daughter."

I call my students "my kids."

Escape from these constructions?

Constructions of the female spirit?

I didn't escape. Not really.

I chose caretaking and taking care,
 biology or not.

Kathleen loves her work teaching theatre and feminist studies at a small Texas university where she encourages young women, through her courses in Feminism and Performance and Theatre for Social Change, to become active in feminist politics, as is she. Frequently, she and her wife, who lives in Los Angeles and is also involved in theatre, team up to stage theatre productions that focus on social change. They fight the good fight together, as she puts it, adding, "I am one happy and lucky woman!"

~ 1963 ~

President Kennedy killed
MLK "I Have a Dream": 200,000 march in D.C.
First human heart transplant, Houston
First liver transplant, Denver
KKK bombs AL church, 4 children killed
Unconstitutional: Prayer in public schools
Jack Ruby shoots Oswald: First live murder on t.v.
Beatlemania sweeps UK
First commercial nuclear reactor: NJ

Song of the Year: I Left My Heart in San Francisco

Films: The Great Escape; Pink Panther; Cleopatra; Hud
Debut: Valium - and not a moment too soon
Beer in a pop-top can
New: Oral polio vaccine on a lump of sugar
First US Lottery – New Hampshire

TV debuts: General Hospital; The Fugitive; Patty Duke Show;
Judy Garland Show; Petticoat Junction
Canceled: Hawaiian Eye; The Real McCoys;
Leave it to Beaver

Born: Brad Pitt; Johnny Depp; Whitney Houston; Edie Falco;
Michael Jordan; Conan O'Brien; Helen Hunt; Benjamin Bratt;
Quintin Tarantino; Andrew Sullivan; Rand Paul

Deaths: Patsy Cline; Sylvia Plath; Edith Piaf; Clifford Odets;
Robert Frost

DAMN!
I FORGOT TO
HAVE CHILDREN

by C K Carman

That was the caption on one of my favorite old t-shirts. The design is a comic-book-style drawing (à la Roy Lichtenstein) of a 1950s-esque woman with her hand pressed dramatically to her forehead, as if she might swoon after realizing she neglected to pick up eggs.

When I wore this (proudly and ironically) shopping, the young female cashiers never seemed to get the joke. Probably because they were experiencing life in the last decade of the 20th century, as women who actually had options—thanks to feminists, including myself, who blazed the trail twenty to thirty years earlier to fight for those options.

These young women didn't feel the need to read *The Feminine Mystique* or *Our Bodies, Ourselves*. They didn't need to join the National Organization for Women (NOW), subscribe to *Ms. Magazine*, or burn their bras. The path to their choices in life had already been cleared by the women of my generation. Women in their twenties, thirties, and forties now choose to marry or not marry, to have careers or be homemakers—or both; to have children or to choose not to have children by use of a plethora of birth control methods, easily accessible now. And they can choose to abort an unwanted pregnancy, thanks to the U.S. Supreme Court's ruling on Roe v. Wade in 1973. At least for now.

But in 1970, women's rights to make choices outside the traditions of the '50s were just coming into my consciousness. And birth control (The Pill had only recently been approved) and the right to an abortion were very far from my mind since I wasn't planning on needing either my first year in college. I was still a virgin, despite the influences of free love and the hippie and anti-war lifestyles. But I became aware soon.

During my first semester in college, I was assigned to a dorm room and a roommate. We were students at Florida State University, and Sarah Weddington, a young Texas attorney, had not yet gone before the Supreme Court to represent a married woman (the "Jane Roe" in Roe v. Wade) and argue for her right to choose an abortion. Ironically, Ms. Weddington was not much older than my roommate and I, and had only just graduated from UT Law School. She is still the youngest attorney to present a case before the Court.

But back at FSU, my roommate got pregnant, and getting an abortion in 1970 wasn't legal in Florida. She had to take a Greyhound bus to New York, alone and without telling her parents, to get an abortion legally. At the time, premarital sex and pregnancy out of wedlock were shocking and shameful, and nobody talked about it. After she returned to FSU, she left school abruptly due to severe post-abortion hemorrhaging. I never saw her again. Soon after, I made an appointment with the only doctor in Tallahassee who would give students prescriptions for The Pill. I didn't want what happened to my roommate to happen to me, when and if I might actually have sex.

In the late 1960s, I was blossoming as a young woman, finishing high school, and looking forward to college. I was an Air Force brat and had lived everywhere from Puerto Rico to Selma, Alabama. The offspring of a military household, I probably had a more liberal and tolerant upbringing than one would suspect due to my exposure to so many different regions, customs, and people, even within my own country, plus a liberal-leaning mother and an absent father off somewhere protecting us from Communism and the Viet

Cong. But as I was entering puberty, I became aware of the real world around me, saw the anti-war riots at the Democratic Convention in Chicago, the civil rights demonstrations in Mississippi, and the triple assassinations of JFK, MLK, and Bobby Kennedy. In my own life, I found I couldn't get a summer job as a lifeguard because I was a girl, even though I was a Certified Water Safety Instructor. And when I worked as a drafts-person in an architectural firm, I had to vacuum the office on Fridays and make coffee in the mornings, even though I was doing the same job as all the drafts-men. When I was trying to break into broadcast journalism, I had to work as a receptionist while I pulled police and fire department reports off the wire and turned them into news stories. It seemed that society kept saying, "you're a girl, you can't do this," but I was also hearing elsewhere (thank you, Helen Reddy), "I can TOO do this, and anything else I want to do, damn it."

The world was changing. I wasn't going off to college to find a husband, as co-eds preceding me might have. Thanks to the Women's Liberation movement, I could choose to be a ballet dancer, major in political science, or study journalism (all my real majors at one time). Unlike my mother's options, which were pretty much limited to marrying and raising a family, I could choose my path in life, and I chose not to marry or have children at that time.

Was my decision made because of a raised feminist consciousness or the invention of The Pill? In other words, which came first, the chicken or the egg? I think having effective and accessible birth control made women's rights more achievable in the 1960s, whereas the suffragette movement in the early 1900s did not coincide with easily accessible birth control. Perhaps the suffragettes were too busy and too exhausted taking care of eight, nine, or ten children—wanted or not. But I had no desire to be tied down by motherhood in my youthful twenties. I could get married and have babies—in that order—if I decided to later. I had too much exploring and living to do while I was young!

But after witnessing my poor college roommate's fate my first month at FSU, I knew pregnancy would derail me from all the experiences awaiting me. My next move was obvious: Get thee to a gynecologist. Get thee on The Pill.

Despite early birth control pills containing enough hormones to choke a horse, they really did change everything. Finally, women could control their own reproduction, and the Sexual Revolution was well on its way. For me and many others, this meant that idle, casual sex was as easy as hailing a cab. It meant we finally could be just like the boys: love 'em and leave 'em. It also meant I had a lot of learning to do.

I'd had little experience or knowledge of sex while growing up, so I was a bit naive in the ways of love. I don't remember much physical affection between my parents, and, remember, my Air Force pilot dad was gone a lot. Maybe because of this, coupled with the changing attitudes and messages being communicated to young women, I decided to explore sex for sex's sake—to be physically intimate with many men but not emotionally intimate with any. Sex with no consequences was very liberating and seemed to make women equal to men, at least in that arena. When Erica Jong's breakthrough book *Fear of Flying* came out, it was more a travel guide to free love and sex for us, and less a novel. It spoke to our many arising conflicts: of womanhood and femininity and love, of our place in society, of our quest for freedom and purpose.

During and after college, I worked as a bartender, crop duster, waitress, draft-person, and—thanks to the FCC mandate for equal opportunity for women and minorities—a radio DJ. Too, as the kids say today, I "hooked up" whenever I wanted, even once during my DJ air shift (thank God for extended cuts of "Stairway to Heaven"). That might have been the time my birth control failed, when, yes, contrary to my carefully planned non-parenthood, the rabbit died. I was pregnant. But I couldn't stop my career to have a child, and the guy who got me pregnant wasn't father or husband material. So after I forced him to fork over half the abortion money (about which he was more concerned than either me or the pregnancy), I found a quaint old doctor who would quietly perform the operation. At least I didn't have to travel alone on a Greyhound bus ten states away, as my college roommate had.

While continuing down my career path, I didn't feel the need to bear children. Having worked in TV news, radio news, and more DJ jobs, I went on to Public Radio in the '80s, and later established a small, local ad agency with two male business partners.

Then, all of a sudden, thirty years later, I realized: Damn! I forgot to have kids! While I was living my exciting life, building a successful business, traveling and doing whatever I wanted, whenever I wanted, such as buying houses or expensive shoes and flying to Zimbabwe to see the total eclipse of the sun, I'd forgotten to find a nice man, get married, and have children.

So was it my destiny to never marry and never have children? Or was I simply in the right place at the right time—or even the wrong place at the right time? If I had been born even ten years earlier, my choices would have been far more limited, as were my mother's.

Do I regret not having children? Sometimes yes, sometimes no. I sometimes think having an adult child would be nice; after all, who's going to take care of me the way I now take care of my ninety-five-year-old mother? Of course, there are no guarantees with children. My child could have been born with major birth defects, developed a drug addiction, died in a foreign war, or just been a ne'er-do-well with no interest in my well being as I grow older.

We live with the choices we make, even the passive ones. In the 1960s and 1970s, a groundswell of feminists opened our eyes to choices we could actively make, controlling reproduction according to our own timing and circumstances. Those young women who didn't see the irony or humor in my t-shirt had no idea that their very jobs and certainly their possibilities for advancement and (almost) equal pay were barely on the country's radar even twenty or so years earlier. They took for granted the trail they were on, knowing little of the women who had blazed it for them: women who marched in the streets, who dared to run for public office and got elected, who pressed against— and even broke—the glass ceilings of their professions, and on whose strong shoulders we now stand. We are all these women. Hear us roar!

CK's broadcast career included TV and radio news, DJ and voice-over work, and jazz programming for Austin's NPR station. After starting an advertising agency, she produced hundreds of radio and TV commercials, and remains the agency's president. She also travels the globe, including Zimbabwe, Libya and the Gobi Desert, to witness total solar eclipses.

A WOMAN IS A WOMAN

by Lin Sutherland

Every week of my adult life, my mother told me I should have a baby.

"Just get pregnant," she'd say. "A woman isn't a woman until she's had a baby."

I would have fallen for this if information to the contrary had not slowly begun to crawl its way out of the cave to American women. Writers such as Betty Friedan talked about "the problem with no name," that is the vast unhappiness and lack of fulfillment of the American housewife; and Gloria Steinem began broadcasting about equal pay and reproductive rights. This was new stuff for the ones whose big sisters had been handed the Father Knows Best/Leave It to Beaver myth on a sparkly, gold-plated platter.

I was a seventeen-year-old virgin when I entered the University of Texas. I'd skipped my senior year in high school because I aced the SAT. In those days, if you were nine and aced the SAT, you could enter college. Coming from an academic family, I knew about The Precursors, all the ones who'd fought hard for women: Susan B. Anthony and the struggle to get the vote; Simone de Beauvoir and Margaret Mead and others who wrote about patriarchal societies and what that meant—barefoot and pregnant. But it was when I signed up for a brand new course called "Women Writers of the 20th Century" that I had my first "click" moment. It came when I read an essay by Virginia Woolf entitled "A Room of One's Own," in which she said that in order to write (or really to do anything) a woman needed a room of her own and some form of her own income. It was like someone had hit me on the head. I thought, "Damn, that makes sense."

My first order of business when I hit the university was to lose my virginity—as soon as possible. I was seventeen and pretty much all my friends had long ago discarded it. Immediately, I let my English Department Teaching Assistant know that I was obliging. I remember little about him except that he was named Joe and was nice. Oh, and this: During coitus, he told me his condom broke. Instantly I leapt up, raced to the bathroom, turned on the tub faucet full-blast and affixed myself to it upside down, legs splayed to the heavens, determined to douche out the little bastards that were fast swimming their way to my ruin. The one thing I had been taught was DON'T GET PREGNANT BEFORE YOU'RE MARRIED. Actually I think it was, "Don't have sex before you're married," but that little detail had fallen by the wayside.

Something was afoot and causing a stir. It was called "The Pill." At the University Health Clinic, where I'd gone in search of same, I was given my first full pelvic examination—by a Catholic doctor, no less—who, upon hearing I'd had two years of Latin, made me conjugate Latin verbs while he inserted the speculum and examined me. "Hic hoc hoc," I recited dutifully, wincing at this new discomfort. "Veni, vinci, vidi." Walking out of the health center with my little packet of pills, I'd wished there was a Latin word for "yahoo!"

Just an aside: It was de rigueur in the '60s for professors and TAs to have sex with their female students. Nobody thought a thing about it.

The Cultural Revolution was in full swing, and it coincided with the formation of the National Organization for Women and the Civil Rights Act, in which a Texas boy succeeded in getting a bill passed that barred employment discrimination for sex, race, etc. Damn, I thought again, all this makes sense, too.

I got busy enjoying one of the most eye-opening, mind-expanding, fun-filled eras in American history—a virtual cornucopia of love-ins, be-ins, brand new music, rising social consciousness, demonstrations against war, broken gender barriers, and worry-free, liberated sex in all its glory. I was free, but also prudent. When I was eighteen, I fell in love with an artist and we lived together for eleven years. We didn't believe in marriage, of course. Why fetter yourself with that? We knew we'd be together for as long as we loved each other, and we did so deeply. We loved each other deeply right up until we separated—which just happened to be around the time I started contemplating having a kid.

So there I was—twenty-nine, single, and on a professional course, working in motion pictures. Each of my relationships lasted about two years but ended before kids could be considered. I met and fell in love with John Steinbeck, the son of the famous writer, and we lived together in Hollywood. He was remarkably funny and smart. "Have his baby!" my mother insisted on the phone from Texas. But I still didn't feel quite ready, with so much fun and adventuring still to do. Also, John had a bit of a drinking problem back then. Nope, not ready for parenting. In the end, after LA burnout, I returned to Texas and began writing. John later died during surgery for his back. What an irony. This brilliant man had survived firefights in Vietnam and the hell of heroin addiction, but he didn't survive American medicine. I was saddened by his death, the loss of a great human being.

"Every week of my adult life my mother told me, 'A woman isn't a woman until she's had a baby.'"

Working hard, I got my foot in the door of travel writing and published several big magazine spreads. Then I got the phone call, not from New York, but from my mother. "Are you EVER going to have a baby?!!" she exclaimed again for the millionth time. "You don't need a man. Just get pregnant." But I didn't want to be a single mother. I'd seen my friends who were single mothers struggling in every way imaginable: young, financially strapped, emotionally overwhelmed, and physically exhausted. I had never eschewed the hard road, but that was one I could choose not to travel. The fact is, deep down, I also believed kids were better off with two parents.

Travel writing took off with the publication of several of my articles in national magazines—a writer's dream of a way to make a living. I savored a decade filled with adventure and exploration. What a delicious, audacious life it was: Kenya, Belize, Morocco, Peru, Brazil, St. Lucia. I saw the American

West by river, soared in hot-air balloons, found giant leatherback tortoises in Costa Rica, sailed a Brigantine, and rode horses in Africa, Ireland, and about a hundred other places. I wouldn't trade my experience for the world.

About the time I hit my forties, my father died and I moved back to the land he left me and my sisters, a little ranch on Onion Creek in South Austin. I made the mistake of revealing that I was perimenopausal. "What?!!" my mother shouted desperately. "Adopt a baby!"

Here is where I should tell you about my extraordinary mother, lest you think hers was a one-verse song. In truth, she was a wonderful role model for me. She had overcome exceptional sexism and restrictions growing up in Charleston, South Carolina. She had wanted twelve boys, but had seven girls. All had kids except for me. My mother graduated *magna cum laude* from College of Charleston, took the $20 gold piece she had won for the math prize and cashed it in on a one-way train ticket west. The fare was $19.30 to Austin, Texas. That's why I'm here, writing in my study, overlooking Onion Creek. If she'd paid $19.30 for a ticket to Timbuktu instead, I'd be there.

My mother married the son of a cowboy who became a university professor; she saved and worked hard and loved her children. Every week she put aside a dollar for our college educations and sent all seven of us to the University of Texas.

When she was sixty, my mother read Steinem and Friedan and soon said "Adios" to Texas, moving to the jungle of British Honduras. There she speculated in jungle land—4,000 acres of it at seven dollars an acre. She built cottages that she sold to hippies who had trundled down in pickup trucks with their dogs, their long-haired "old ladies," and their diaper-less kids. My mother traveled the countryside by herself, donning a little red backpack. She was a one-woman force to be reckoned with: strong, stubborn, fearless, funny, highly intelligent, who—a product of her times—always believed every woman should have kids. At sixty-five, she adopted a baby! He was an eight-week-old, born on the island she called home. At last—the little boy she'd never birthed. Her friends were stunned. "Are you crazy?!" they wailed. "When he's fifteen, you'll be eighty! When he's twenty-five, you'll be ninety!"

And so she was.

My mother died on the island at the age of ninety-three. Her son, my little brother, was twenty-eight and loved her dearly.

On the day before she died, I sat next to her bed stroking the little dog by her side, my other hand resting on hers. For years this woman had infuriated me and driven me crazy, but losing her was breaking my heart. "I love you, Mama," I said. She replied, "I love you. I love all my daughters"—as we knew she always had. Then she paused and looked out at the swaying palm fronds, listening to the tidal breeze, and spoke her last words to me.

"Honey, do what you want to do. A woman is a woman no matter what."

Lin is a writer and horse rancher at her home, Onion Creek Ranch, in Austin, TX. She writes personal memoir, creative non-fiction, poetry and travel adventure. She has published for 35 years in national and regional anthologies.

"If you bungle raising your children, I don't think whatever else you do well matters very much."

Jacqueline Kennedy Onassis

TIMING

by Jane Burkett

Of *course* I was gonna have lots of babies when I grew up! Although my mother never worked, some did, so what if I wanted a career, too? Hmm… teacher, secretary or nurse? Easy: nurse.

But no way was I gonna take care of sick people—I knew they were no fun. Well, Daddy made me laugh, so I might've taken care of him; but whenever my big sister and brother got sick, they vomited—and how much fun is that? I don't remember Mother ever vomiting, but, good grief, she was sick all the time. I wasn't sure *what* she had.

I saw on *I Love Lucy*, when little Ricky was born, the kind of nurse I wanted to be. The kind who takes care of the new babies. That really looked like fun. I just loved babies.

In grade school, I gave a lot of thought to babies—and even more thought to what life was like as they got older. Thanks to some keen powers of observation and an abundance of logic, by the time I was nine or so I'd developed a theory on the subject. Probably around the time Daddy had to break the bathroom window to get Mother out. That was pretty scary, but when I asked him what was wrong and he said something about gas I figured she must've had a really bad stomach ache. Anyway, what I decided about babies was that when I finally had my own, I'd keep it for as long as it was cute and cuddly. Then, at about five, I'd throw it away and get me another little bitty one.

Was the reason I never had children that my mother made me feel disposable when I was five? The more I was able to do for myself the less she seemed interested in me. I had to wonder if all children beyond the toddler stage were no longer lovable.

Was my decision the result of finally realizing what a giant pain in the neck children were? Seriously, what fool in her right mind would spend a minute more than she absolutely had to with the annoying little things? Mother made it clear there were far more exciting things one could do with her time: like bridge club twice a month and drinks every afternoon with friends and dinner parties at the Country Club. There was television. There was solitaire.

Had Mother's incessant criticism, always demanding, never satisfied, instilled in me a belief I wasn't good enough?

What about the alcoholism? A parent who is drunk is absent even if you're together in

❋❋❋❋❋❋❋❋❋❋❋❋

"Given the similarities in our early years, I'm convinced Mother's path and mine diverged when we were young adults primarily because of what was different: the vast disparity in opportunities available to each of us."

❋❋❋❋❋❋❋❋❋❋❋❋

the same room. When they're both drunk, you're home alone. Was this the basis for my deep-seated fear of abandonment? Mother's repeated suicide attempts, beginning the day she turned on the gas and lay on the bathroom floor, were only part of that equation.

What about her volatility? The way she'd fly off the handle at the drop of a hat? More often than not these outbursts were followed by bouts of depression so debilitating she could barely get out of bed. Surely that roller coaster fed my insecurities and heightened my dread of being like her, equally unfit to raise children.

Why hadn't Daddy done more to protect us? Was his reluctance to confront her on our behalf at the root of my nagging distrust of men and my suspicions about marriage altogether?

Was any one of these issues the reason I didn't have children? Were they collectively the reason? No. They shaped me and left me wounded, but they did not dictate the entirety of my journey. If such an upbringing were the driving factor that steered me from motherhood, why, then, did my mother have me?

In significant ways Mother's childhood was much like mine. She was born to a demanding, hypercritical woman, easily stressed. My grandfather was even less inclined toward confrontation than my father and equally inept at shielding his five children from their mother's angry moods. As a young man my grandfather had a drinking problem, although my take-charge grandmother had put her foot down and, for the most part, he abstained. Mama and Papa weren't wealthy, but many of their friends were, and my grandmother, too, was more suited to socializing than to mothering. Her maternal instincts didn't kick in until she had grandchildren. Of her three daughters who had children, only the youngest was even remotely maternal. To say that my mother and her siblings struggled as adults with issues of insecurity, addiction and anger would be an understatement.

Given the similarities in our early years, Mother's path and mine diverged when we were young adults primarily because of what was different: the vast disparity in opportunities available to each of us. If Auntie Mame was right when she said, 'Life's a banquet' then Mother and I had been handed two very different menus. Mine was from Alice's Restaurant with its promise: You Can Have Anything You Want. By contrast, Mother's menu offered choices so limited and lackluster it might well have come from the lunch counter at Woolworth's.

When I, the youngest child, went away to college, my parents began living alone for the first time since they'd married twenty-five years earlier. By then Mother was under psychiatric care, married to a man who found personal introspection an alien concept, as did most men of his era. Drinking was Daddy's preferred method for dealing with stress. Now in her mid-forties, Mother was a woman with little self-confidence and precious few choices but to accept what lay ahead: a road worn to a rut by women who had traveled it for decades.

Just weeks before I left home, the National Organization for Women was founded.

As the Women's Movement made news and continued to gain steam, did

Mother start to feel she was somehow trapped on the dull side of a coin? Did she realize that its other side, the side facing me, was being burnished to a sparkly sheen by a defiant band of upstarts who were telling the women of my generation to reach for the sky?

After five years, one early Christmas morning, Mother died at the age of fifty from a self-inflicted gunshot wound. The next day was my twenty-fourth birthday. Weeks later and 400 miles away, on a sidewalk in San Marcos, Texas, director Sam Peckinpah hired me to be Ali MacGraw's stand-in on *The Getaway,* starring her and Steve McQueen. What lay before me was anything but a rut—it was a road to adventure, the likes of which my funny, intelligent mother would have loved if she'd had the same options as I when she was 24. Maybe she'd have passed on the skydiving, but I bet she gladly would have traipsed from England to Mykonos with only a duffle bag, especially if the person who lugged it when it got too heavy was a handsome young law-yer studying at Cambridge. Would she have wanted a dream job at a luxury hotel in the French Quarter and a chance to work on films in Los Angeles? Of course! And maybe buying and remodeling homes, as I did in Austin , would have been an outlet for her immense creativity. Mother married and had children because that was the expected path for most women born prior to the 1960s. But she was no more wired to be a mother than I was. I believe the explanation for our very different journeys comes down to timing. By no more than the luck of the draw, my birthday came twenty-six years after hers.

I was—and am—the fortunate one.

After twenty years of remodeling, Jane picked up some pastels and began painting. A voracious reader, she also designs, writes, cooks sumptuous meals for her friends – and marches in protest of idiot lawmakers, just as she did in the '60s.

~ 1964 ~

Congress authorizes war against N. Vietnam

LBJ signs Civil Rights Act of 1964

Captured: The Boston Strangler

Name-change: Cassius Clay = Mohammad Ali

Largest quake in US history: 9.2, Alaska

The Mods and the Rockers rumble in Britain

US: Race riots in Harlem

World's Fair: New York

Nelson Mandela: life sentence

S. Africa banned from Tokyo Summer Olympics

Nobel Peace Prize: Martin Luther King

Sidney Poitier makes history: Best Actor

Warren Commission Report: Oswald acted alone

Rolling Stones: first album

Bob Dylan: The Times They Are a-Changing

73 million watch Beatles on The Ed Sullivan Show

13 simultaneous Beatles hits on Billboard's Top 100

Sony debuts the first VCR

Ford introduces the Mustang

Debuts: Computer mouse; Buffalo wings; bubble wrap

TV debut: Peyton Place w/Mia Farrow, Ryan O'Neal

Movies: Zorba the Greek; A Shot in the Dark;
Tom Jones

Song of the Year: Days of Wine and Roses

Largest US publication: S & H Green Stamps Catalogue

WHERE DID THE TIME GO?

by Meg Wilson

I forgot to have kids. No big deal. Been crazy busy. What's that all about?!

When I was working in the governor's office, my husband used to call my boss to ask if he could make a date with his wife. Cute, but true. I was living the dream. I had it all: a great job, a great husband, lots of friends, important volunteer and political efforts, promotions in the offing. We were out to save the world—or at least one corner of it. Kids? Who had time? Not me—at least not then. As it turned out, not ever.

My mother had attended Duke University where she got a degree in biology and planned to go to medical school. But her family's finances didn't allow for graduate school. Instead, she went to work as a research chemist for Esso, which is where she met my father. After they were married, she quit her job. She bought into the whole package of the '50s: husband, kids, housewife. Why? The lifestyle suited her, and, being frighteningly efficient, she could take care of four kids and the house and still have time left for herself. She loved to read, garden, swim, and volunteer with the local women's club. When she read the *Feminine Mystique,* she was amazed Betty Friedan had nailed it so well. Without indulging in self-pity, she was sure it had been written for her.

My mother and her mother were both fans of Margaret Sanger, the US pioneer of birth control distribution. When each of us kids reached puberty, my mother gave us the *Red Cross Handbook,* telling us to read the section on reproduction. If my brothers ever got a girl pregnant, she told them, they'd be at fault, not the girl! Contraception was out there—use it!

Instead of a lecture, I got the biology, an introduction to menstruation and the underlying expectation to be a "good girl." But "good" wasn't exactly the norm in Arcola, Illinois, at the time. There, normal often looked like pregnant, marry, graduate high school, or some combination. I knew only one high school girl who, despite having a child, went on to college unmarried.

Growing up in a small town with my parents and three brothers was idyllic, a perfect place to be a kid. But it didn't seem to offer much beyond childhood. By seeing how our parents would become restless, living in the middle of corn fields, the narrowness of the local horizon seeped into our kid-consciousness. I think I'd have steered clear of reckless behavior guaranteed to hold me there, even if we hadn't moved.

But we did move—big time, to Brussels, Belgium, when I was eleven. My chemical engineer father, who'd contributed to the invention of polyethylene, was wooed to return to Esso to work at a new plastics research lab there. I, who was terrified of the big city of Champaign, Illinois, landed in the middle of a huge, foreign city, thrown into a new life.

As our parents thrived in cosmopolitan Brussels, we kids were free to explore a wholly new world. This was a different kind of idyllic: The International School of Brussels excelled at academics, and girls were expected to do just as well as the boys, no matter what the subject. I was thrilled by the intellectual challenge and dove into my classes with glee and determination.

In Brussels, my mother kicked back a bit as the four of us were old enough to take care of ourselves, mostly. I got a motorcycle so I could be more mobile. Riding the bus was okay, but to be active in sports and clubs, my Honda Supersport gave me freedom! I could hang out with friends scattered all over Brussels, and could also over-commit to extracurricular activities, beginning a lifelong proclivity to saying, "Yes" instead of "No."

I babysat a lot in high school, one of the few ways I could earn money in a foreign country. I remember one lady I worked for who said that she loved her three boisterous children, but if she had it to do all over again, she wouldn't have kids.

My friends and I seemed to be the only "grownups" she talked to other than her husband. Bitter undertones, loneliness, and a hint of hopelessness were constants in her conversations with us. Their context and content were radical to me and rattled my young brain.

Having a motorcycle enabled me to go where I wanted and that often meant to the Grand Place in Brussels for mulled wine and *frites* with the school crowd. It wasn't much of a step beyond that to take in the new '60s music and explore dating and sex.

Sex without birth control was nerve wracking in this very Catholic country where birth control was difficult to get. So I stole my father's condoms. Remembering my Red Cross reading, I used the rhythm method and withdrawal for my backup plans.

Beyond wanting me to go to college, my parents' expectations were vague. My dear father, philosophically a libertarian but domestically a traditionalist, wanted me to go to college, find a husband, graduate and have kids—carrying forward the Arcola High School's model to college! I explained that I was going to college for an education, nothing else.

I arrived in New York to attend Ithaca College. There, the first thing I did was register, changing from my declared major, biology, to politics. The second thing I did was find the health center for a prescription for The Pill. My academic program was exhilarating, mixing politics and science. I immersed myself and even helped get a radical, socialist, feminist professor hired by the department. My social life was just as thrilling—no holds barred. I was becoming an aggressive feminist; sexual relations were always on my terms. Birth control removed the fear, letting me have it all.

I met a wonderful man from Cornell when I was a junior, a true love. Unfortunately, he was Catholic, his parents extremely so. Even then, I had an inkling I didn't want kids, but certainly not right away. Well, he needed to have kids—for his parents! We never married.

By the time I was a senior, I was a committed political feminist. After graduation, I planned to acquire the necessary skills to bend public policy to better serve the future—a feminist future, a science-smart future, one that included ZPG (zero population growth), education for all, equal rights for women around the world and participation by women at all levels in politics. I was world-wise and full of confidence.

The LBJ School of Public Affairs at UT Austin admitted me into their master's program with a full scholarship. I was off to Texas with no need for parental financial support. I was launching my dream career.

A research project I worked on in graduate school required my interviewing several elderly women. I met one in a rural area some thirty miles outside Austin. Among her many tales about growing up in Texas, the most surprising was hearing her say that she didn't know until late in life there was any other form of birth control than menopause! I hadn't expected to get into that topic with her, but clearly she wanted to talk, to warn a young woman to be smarter than she'd been when getting married! If only she had known.

Over the summer between my first and second years at the LBJ School, I sat myself down and asked what I wanted out of life. I had racked up many experiences in my short life, but I needed to decide what would make my future my own—not one that just happened to me. I made two life-changing decisions: First, I decided I wanted a monogamous, heterosexual, faithful, permanent relationship. Second, I decided that I would never work in the field of social services for a living. I would only work in a field where there were real answers, which meant my work would center on science and technology. My first decision was startling to me and also to my friends who barely recognized the woman expressing such a traditional view of relationships. But I had kissed a lot of frogs and none had been my prince. Now I wanted a real partner, and I was finally ready to commit to one.

My feminism spurred me to sign up for a VW repair class at the Community Auto Co-Op. I was determined not to get ripped off every time I took my car for repairs, as had happened in my first term of graduate school. It seemed the perfect thing to do the summer before my second year. I got a call from a guy named Fred Chriswell: The class would begin the following Saturday; bring paper towels and mosquito spray and wear comfortable clothes. Over four weekends, we were to learn the basics in VW maintenance. However, because I had the opportunity to testify before the newly formed Austin Commission on the Status of Women, I was going to miss one class. Fred offered to give me a make-up class on tune-ups one Friday if I would give him a ride to the brake shop. He needed to get his car ready for a driving vacation.

What should have been a simple two- to three-hour transaction turned into an entire day of quirky twists and turns. At the brake shop, Fred was told they'd take only cash, so we had to leave and go to the drive-thru at his bank. Back at the brake shop, after Fred gave me the tune-up class, we started working on his brakes when he realized he needed traveler's checks for his trip. So we drove back to the bank. But for traveler's checks we had to go inside. Friday afternoon, payday for many, made the place crowded. As a rule, Fred hates standing in lines. That day he didn't seem to mind. It was nearly 7 p.m. p.m. when I finally I headed home, ever so reluctantly.

Fred went on his vacation, telling friends along the way about the amazing woman he'd just met. They said, "And you left town?!" I received several postcards while he was away and a phone call the minute he got back. We dated through the rest of the summer. For Halloween, I'd gotten invitations to parties, but after going to the first I decided I'd rather go trick or treating on my own. I stood at Fred's doorstep in a black velvet dress, and granny glasses with my hair powdered white. In my purse was my diaphragm. "Trick or treat!" He was happily surprised to see me. It was a treat!

In January I moved in with him. That summer we had a late-night conversation about what we wanted to do with each other when we were in our sixties. I said, "Don't

"I had it all: a great job, a great husband, lots of friends, important volunteer and political efforts, promotions in the offing. We were out to save the world — or at least one corner of it. Kids? Who had time?"

you think that means we should get married?" After peeling himself off the ceiling, Fred agreed that marriage was a fine idea. None of our musings or plans included kids.

In November, the day after Halloween, we got married. Soon after, I eagerly took him to meet my maternal grandmother. Upon hearing we had no plans to have children, she said, "Why bother getting married?" That twisted my brain. Surely she wasn't suggesting I just live with him—she'd never have approved of that! Then, when I told her I hadn't taken Fred's name, Granny Gray, with her hands on her hips, glared at him, "Damn it, man! Stand up for your rights! Make her take your name!" My wonderful husband just smiled and shook his head.

I had found a man who wanted the tradition of fidelity and permanence, but with no desire to box me in. He admired my career dreams and supported my extracurricular activities even though they took time away from us. He accepted the fact that I had compulsions to over-commit to causes I believe in.

My success allowed Fred to find his way, from garage mechanic, camera repairman, and telemedicine R&D manager to firmware manager for battery technology at Texas Instruments. A late bloomer, Fred was given the time he needed to realize his potential.

Fred and I were happy without kids. But by our mid-thirties, we were slowing down.

Maybe it was time to rethink the matter, then wham! I was diagnosed with eye cancer and, because cancer is sensitive to pregnancy hormones, I was advised against getting pregnant. Fred was adamant: He'd rather have me than a kid! Case closed. For my fortieth birthday, I got my tubes tied.

Recently a friend exclaimed, "I know why you and Fred are so happy! You don't have kids." I had to agree. We enjoy spending our time on projects, traveling, sharing with one another what we've read, cooking for ourselves as well as for friends, and supporting causes. We are defined by our relationship with each other—not by a life lived through kids. While some of our friends are envious that we spend so much quality time together —for thirty-seven years now—I sometimes wonder what life would look like if we'd had children. We had thought we had all the time in the world to make that decision, until we didn't.

Life is perversely inverted: We should be crazy-busy when we're young, then have kids when we're older. Then, when our bodies can no longer make them, we can contribute our time and patience to them, when our minds are overflowing with life to share with them.

Meg teaches Technology Commercialization in Mexico, through IC2, at The University of Texas at Austin. She's an avid weaver and active in weaving and fiber organizations. Her other interests include politics, economics, gardening and her hubby, Fred.

~ 1965 ~

Av cost of new home: $13,500
Gas: 31 cents/gal
Gold: $36/oz
First US combat troops to Vietnam
35,000 protesters march on Washington
Selma riots: 2,600 arrested, including MLK
Watts Riots: 4,000 arrested, 34 dead, 1,000 injured
USSR: first space-walk by man
Summer debut: Mini-skirt, UK
Twiggy: fashion sensation, UK
Hurricane Betsy: $1B damage to Bahamas/Fla/La
Pope Paul VI: first pope to visit US
First US airlifts out of Cuba
Sold-out in 17 minutes: Beatles at Shea Stadium
Grateful Dead: first concert, San Francisco

Songs: *Mamas & The Papas: Go Where You Wanna Go*

Record of the Year: *Girl from Ipanema*

TV debuts: *The Dating Game; Dean Martin Show*

Born: *J. K. Rowling; Sarah Jessica Parker; Ben Stiller; Robert Downey, Jr.; Kyra Sedgwick; Brooke Shields*

Deaths: *Winston Churchill; T.S. Eliot; Nat King Cole*

CHARGED BY
A GALLOPING RHINO

by Mary-Ellen Campbell

The ranger puts a finger to his lips, points to a nearby tree, and gestures for me to climb high up in it. With a rush of adrenaline, video camera in hand, amazingly, I scale the tree as the rhino picks up our scent and charges toward us. Circling our safe haven, he snorts irascibly and stays for too long a time. Finally, a bull elephant comes running at him, chasing him away.

I captured it all on tape, hoping to use the footage in my video productions focused on the Arts of Asia. In my travels, I've experienced many similar "rushes," such as the time I unearthed a 2,500-year-old piece of Greek pottery on an archeological site in Israel and the times I scoured the darkness watching for hyenas' eyes while camping overnight in the South African bush. If I had chosen to have children and raise a family over exploring the world, would I have had any of these adventures? In the absence of familial distractions, I have been free to immerse myself in some of nature's most alluring settings, meet people from an array of cultures, and explore distant cities.

When she was angry with me for some infraction, Mother would tell me,

"Never have children." She was upset at that moment that I was less than the perfect child. Little did she know how I would take her message to heart. I disregarded many of her edicts, but that one stuck.

My choice not to have children wasn't based solely on my mother's advice. I made the decision because of my competitive, ambitious nature and the circumstances of my adult life. As a second-generation American, born in New York City, raised on Long Island, and the first in my family to attend University, I was encouraged from an early age to be the best I could be in school, at art, at dancing, etc. I took up many extracurricular activities and, when I wasn't studying, was an avid reader. Reading was my escape from boring, comfortable suburbia. It transported me to places I'd never seen and beckoned me to try things beyond the parochial life I was living. Like a sponge, I soaked up tales in books and plays from over the centuries, stories that took me from the Pacific Islands to outer space. Such was my world for my first eleven years. That's when my sister was born. A surprise, I

"The years I spent as a single woman have been the best of my life. "

think. Suddenly life wasn't centered on me. Because my mother worked part-time, it fell to me to take care of Alison when I got home from school. I loved my baby sister. What I did not love were the constraints on my time she posed. I made a mental note: This is what raising a child is like.

From 1964 to 1968, I lived at home, working part-time teaching dance where I got a dose of "kids." I attended St. John's University on full scholarship. My university years were filled with fun, friends, and boys. After graduating, I prepared to go to Michigan State for my master's.

The summer before leaving for grad school, I had an affair with a former painting instructor. He was nineteen years older than I, a suave and talented artist, never without a cigarette dangling from his thin French lips. It was supposed to be a fling—this was the late '60s after all. But it quickly became a serious relationship. For the year I was in Michigan, we secretly saw each other on holidays and spoke nightly. The day after I graduated, we boarded a plane together and flew to France. My mother nearly had a nervous breakdown. This was not supposed to happen to her nice Catholic daughter. In France we visited his family, who only marginally accepted me.

No one expected ours to be more than a summer romance. But we stayed together, partly because I was naïve, largely because he loved attention from an adoring younger woman.

Upon our return to the US, I began my stint as an art teacher, first in grade school and then in junior high and high school. I learned that not all kids like creating art and that motivating them can be difficult. After three years, I quit teaching in order to begin a career as a graphic designer, having only myself to motivate. My French husband, whom I'd married after years of living together, helped me get started with freelance design work through his connections. When I later landed a full-time job, I started at the bottom. My ambition and talent moved me forward, each new job better than the last. But I was working fifty-one weeks of the year and putting in a lot of overtime. In what little spare time was left, I created my own art. There was no time for babies.

Regardless of what you may have heard about Frenchmen, our sex life was never that great. My husband, Claude, a professor, had summers off and went to France for five weeks each year to visit his parents. It was during one of those summers that I had an affair with a co-worker who was closer to my age. Still in my twenties, I was lonely, with little experience or experimentation behind me. My penchant for risk-taking came out in the intrigue and machinations of my affair.

After two years, Claude got wise and moved to end an already dead marriage. He told me I no longer "inspired" him. I suspect what bothered him was that I no longer "adored" him. For inspiration, he turned instead to younger student models. By then I was a successful designer, soon to become a college professor myself.

I'd seen up close what a great life my husband led: a lot of free time to create, summers off to travel. It motivated me to work hard as a designer and to use my success as a springboard to becoming a professor. I set my sights on finding a college where graphic design programs were just beginning to take off. After both my marriage and the affair ended, I applied for a position in Jersey City, NJ, across the river from Manhattan and the New York art scene.

It was while I was still married to Claude that I discovered a passion for the outdoors, taking up hiking, biking, skiing, camping—all of which my artist husband disdained. One day on a hike on Long Island, I met Charlie, the man who would become my second husband. He was handsome, only one year older, and loved being outdoors, too. I fell fast and hard. After dating for six months, we moved in together. I know now it was a rebound relationship, one that included his ten-year-old son, making me an instant stepmother. His son's biological mother, living in Virginia, had little initial impact on our new family except with occasional phone calls. Charlie proved to be a very strict and dictatorial father who, always shouting, meted out the same measure of punishment regardless of the crime.

I made another mental note: Charlie would never be the father of a child of mine. But a year after living together and having started my university teaching job, I got pregnant. Also, I'd begun studying for yet another degree to better my chances for the security that comes with having tenure, so the timing couldn't have been worse. My husband wasn't thrilled being a father to the child he had and he'd indicated he didn't want other children, so I decided to terminate the pregnancy. Less than a week later, Charlie got a vasectomy, thus ending the likelihood I would ever have his child.

My stepson lived with us until he was sixteen, when he moved back with his mother for a year before being sent to boarding school. As his stepmother, I did a decent job, but it was his father who made the major decisions as to his upbringing. I do believe I provided him the only stability in his young life and was a role model for tolerance and promoting art and literature. He went on to study writing and filmmaking.

My decision to be childless was the right one for me. Charlie and I remained married for sixteen years, the last one of which was hell. If we'd chosen to have the baby, he/she would have been a teenager when our marriage was falling apart. I consider it a blessing the child didn't have to endure that turmoil. In addition to Charlie's terrible temper, he was also an alcoholic, though he never admitted it. After trying counseling and going to Al-Anon myself for four years, I called it quits and got a divorce. I was fifty years old and, for the first time in my life, free to go where I wanted, when I wanted.

These years as a single woman have been the best of my life. I've continued to work, achieving full professorship and several prestigious grants. Beginning with that first trip to France in 1969, I've loved traveling. I've trekked to sixty countries many of them several times over where I have worked, lived, and explored. I've created my art all over the United States and abroad and made many friends along the way. I've had a few lovers to make up for the time in my early life when I didn't shop around. But I haven't found the one person to share my very complicated life now. I do have several people sharing different parts of it, and that seems to work best for me.

I still enjoy the outdoors—and chasing large animals in Asia and Africa.

Mary-Ellen recently retired after 34 years as a Professor of Art at a university in New Jersey. When not traveling around the world for fun, teaching workshops, volunteering on various projects, or as an artist-in-residence, she splits her time between her apartment in New York City where she enjoys the arts and dancing and her country retreat in upstate NY where she kayaks, hikes, skis, makes her art and plans her next adventure.

FRUITLESS IN THE BIG APPLE

by Karen Kreps

Seven miscarriages occurred between my brother's birth and mine. I was that wanted child. My parents were children of Eastern European Jews who came to New York a century ago. My brother would carry on our family name, though he'd marry out of the tribe. Since Jewish heritage runs maternally, I would carry on the faith.

My mother wanted nothing more than for her children and grandchildren to be happy. She expected I'd be happy when I grew up, got married, and had children who would be the raison d'être of my life, as it had been for her.

I didn't know the raison d'être of my life, though I searched in philosophy, psychology, astrology, palmistry, spirituality, and Yoga. Synagogue had given me an empty experience, my family being barely observant. I longed for a sense of belonging, of fitting in, of connecting. As a teen in the 1960s in New York, that meant being a non-conformist. I wanted to conform and not conform at the same time.

My parents enrolled me in a progressive private school, but made it clear they expected me to be a conventional virgin bride. With my classmates on

The Pill or getting pregnant, this seemed rather unlikely.

Counterculture called. Observing the material pettiness of post-war Americans made me squirm. Around the dinner table, I longed for meaningful dialogue, not superficial small talk. I went to the first "Be-In" in Central Park's Sheep Meadow. Later, I joined friends and teachers and marched up Fifth Avenue in the first major protest against the Vietnam War. I tried pot and hash and heavy petting with long-haired boys in the park after school.

But in 1967, before my "deflowering" would occur, I met my guru. Through Yoga, I found myself more interested in discovering my Higher Self than in meeting boys. To my father, the swami was an evil Pied Piper, leading his rebellious daughter away from the morals of his forebears. Dad didn't realize that Yoga actually served to shelter me from the era's rapidly changing social norms.

Contraceptives were as easy for my crowd to get as soft drugs and psychedelics. People turned on, tuned in, and followed a different drummer. My high school joined the student strike against the war in support of Columbia University twenty blocks away, where protesters took over the administration building and made national headlines. Posters for peace, flower power, and "Make Love Not War" competed with posters showing the angry-fist logo of the Black Panthers. There were race riots in Harlem. When smoke billowed from not-too-distant tenement fires, I escaped the chaos by lighting incense in my bedroom and meditating for peace.

At age eighteen, two days after my high-school graduation, I moved out of my parents' Upper East Side apartment, taking the cross-town bus to the birthplace of Integral Yoga. The posters said, "The door is open to meet Swami Satchidananda. And, when you leave, you may find another door is open." And many did, though never in exactly the way I had pictured.

Wanting to help bring Integral Yoga to the western world, I shared a room with two other yoginis and commuted to NYU, rather than live in a dorm like a normal co-ed. Whether out of fear of competing in the procreative marketplace or due to a true spiritual calling, a Bohemian craving led me to contemplate renouncing all worldly things, becoming a swami with a shaved head and orange caftan, practicing celibacy, and forgoing family. This seemed a noble and lofty goal, to sacrifice having a husband and children in order to be of service to a greater community, the planet, and God.

But two years later my hormones kicked in. Even as I directed my energy into Hatha Yoga, I read in *Life* magazine about the Sexual Revolution that was sweeping the nation. When sexual desire awoke within me, I saw it also as a sign of my spiritual weakness. I descended into my own Dark Night of the Soul, ashamed. Before I could fully commit to a celibate life, I wanted to know what it was I was giving up. I moved out of the ashram and attended graduate school in Greenwich Village, entering the world of publishing. I channeled my energies into environmental activism, using my mothering energy to mother the Earth. I fought plans for development of nearly 3,000 forested acres in the Hudson Valley, which later, thankfully, were added to a state park instead. I taught Yoga, nurturing the creative spiritual evolvement of my students in weekly classes. And I began to date.

"Contraceptives were as easy for my crowd to get as soft drugs and psychedelics."

One-night stands came easily for many, but not for me. Men ran the other way when I made it known that I didn't take lightly the prospect of losing my "cherry." It wasn't until I was twenty-one, while traveling, that I first gained carnal knowledge in a loving and memorable way.

When I wasn't vainly trying to save the world, my thoughts on marriage were, at best, incidental. Orgasms were what mattered, and for those there were weekends in the country, South Hampton beach-shares, and Club Med getaways. If I didn't have a date, a friend and I might drive down the streets of SoHo late at night looking for lively parties to crash. The perks that came with my editorial jobs gave me entry to new Broadway shows, new discothèques such as Studio 54, and glamorous receptions. All I needed was an escort, and they were plentiful.

I had a long string of relationships, many of them monogamous, with older commitment-phobic men, far more worldly than I. After I lived with a Vietnam vet for two years, his job instability led to our breakup and my subsequent relief that we hadn't made the mistake of tying the knot and having children.

In the publishing world, my head bumped the glass ceiling. I was indefatigable as I strove for professional recognition and equal pay in a patriarchal world. At the same time, I was free to find ways beyond having children to express the divine feminine aspect of my being. Journaling and writing an advice column let me nurture ideas I could share. I relished gathering in women's circles, sharing deeply, and performing rituals that attuned me to both biological and planetary cycles. Noticing the bewitching effect I had on men awakened a new source for feeling empowered and creative.

Ever on the lookout for Mr. Right but between serious relationships, I took comfort with standby lovers. These men couldn't be counted on as faithful partners, but at least they were available when I didn't want to sleep alone. And when they weren't, thanks to the freedom unleashed by feminism, such substitutes as dildos and Ben Wa balls came in handy. Physical intimacy was plentiful, but still I longed for emotional intimacy on a deeper level.

In my thirties, I focused on my career and attended workshops focused on finding happiness—with or without a man. Yet every month, as I endured heavy bleeding and cramps, I knew that time was running out for me to get pregnant. In the absence of a husband, a good husband, I never considered having a child. My income barely covered my grungy little apartment, a place hopelessly too small for raising a child. As the clock ticked, news of a woman having her first child late in life gave me hope. Advances in modern science pushed higher the age for childbearing. Still, I was conflicted, unsure I would ever want a child. As someone who couldn't stand to babysit other people's children, would I ever possess the patience needed to take care of my own?

While working near the skating rink at Rockefeller Center, I decided to take up ice dancing. I loved my pro—but he was gay. I began to think that all the men in my neighborhood were gay. *New York* magazine even had a cover story bemoaning the dismal ratio of straight women to straight men. Then, in 1985, a close friend from grad school died suddenly, the victim of an early case of AIDS. Before long, death seemed to roam the streets of Greenwich Village, gripping us with wrenching fear and bringing my sexual exploration to a screeching halt. For years I'd thought of sex as a grand adventure, a symphony playing the background theme to my life. Now, any man with whom I slept posed a lethal threat.

I fought lonely despair by practicing Yoga and skating and pouring my energy into my work, now editing online rather than for print. Five years later, I invited a co-worker and her boyfriend to join me one afternoon to go skating on a frozen pond. They brought along a friend, introducing me to the man who would become my husband of twenty-one years—and counting.

As he and I grew close enough to broach the subject of children, we were open to the idea, but also ambivalent. No rush, we'd take it up after we got married. But nine months after our beautiful wedding, it was a pink slip, not a baby, that changed our lives. The corporation that had promised my well-educated spouse life-long security was downsizing. We were stunned.

From New York, my husband's career took us to Austin, Texas. Leaving the only place I'd ever called home caused wrenching trauma that took two years to subside to the point where I could even consider stopping contraceptive use for the first time. By then I was forty-three and our efforts were fruitless. Only briefly did we consider fertility treatments or adoption. Mostly relieved not to get pregnant, I was also tinged with guilt, symbolizing a dead branch on the family tree, a disappointment to my ancestors.

Eventually, my father wrote me off as genetically unviable and decided to leave the lion's share of his property to my procreative brother. It would be my mother, may she rest in peace, who finally let me off the hook. I'll never forget the day she secretly confided in me that, while she'd always hoped I'd get married and have children, she saw that I had other options that clearly gave meaning to my life. If I was happy, she was happy.

I often thank my lucky stars that my husband and I were spared the responsibility of parenthood. Many of my friends' lives revolved around raising their children, which burdened them with debts I feel fortunate not to have incurred. I had far more personal flexibility than did they. Being childless has allowed my husband and me the freedom to travel the world and more easily focus on our own aspirations. I have learned to "mother" in a different way. Instead of sharing emotional intimacy with a child, I share it in my writing and in communion with others, with animals, with the Earth.

Have I regrets? Who doesn't? But looking at the havoc mankind has wrought upon the planet, I admit to being grateful no children or grandchildren of mine must face the ever-increasing threats to the environment. Yet, genetics indicate I will outlive my husband. Had I had a child, would he or she have looked after me in my old age?

All those years ago, I began a search for a way that I could be of service to the greater community, the planet, or God. Did I find it? I believe I have made a slight, yet significant, difference in many people's lives. I am blessed to have been born when I was, I love the life I lead, and I continue to discover ways to express my purpose.

Without children to serve as my raison d'être, I've been free to find a different purpose. I've come to see myself as a privileged, invited guest at a wonderful party called Life. My purpose is to be what, to me, is a good guest. That means showing up, getting along with the other guests, being ready to play whatever games the host provides, and cleaning up after myself. There's no need to leave behind more than the small imprints I've made on the lives I've touched.

Living in Austin, Texas, Karen is the owner of Net Ingenuity, producing custom WordPress websites. Year round she swims daily in the chilly, invigorating waters of Barton Springs and, along with her husband, looks forward to nurturing to an old age their second pair of cats.

~ 1966 ~

Av cost of new home: $14,200
New car: $2,650
Gas: 32 cents/gal
New dishwasher: $120
First-class stamp: 5 cents
FDA: The Pill is safe
New: Medicare
Billie Jean King wins Wimbledon
Kevlar invented by Dupont chemist, Stephanie Kwolek
Miranda decided by Supreme Court
DNA code deciphered by MIT biochemist
Ronald Reagan: Gov. of California
CBS won't air Psycho: too violent for in-home audience
Astrodome completed in Houston
National Organization of Women founded in NY

TV debut: *Star Trek*

Best Picture: *Sound of Music*
Others: Dr. Zhivago; The Chase; Who's Afraid of Virginia Woolf?; A Man and a Woman

Songs: *Simon and Garfunkel: Sounds of Silence*
Monday, Monday makes Mamas & Papas a global sensation

Deaths: *Walt Disney, age 64*
Charles Whitman kills 14 on UT campus in Austin

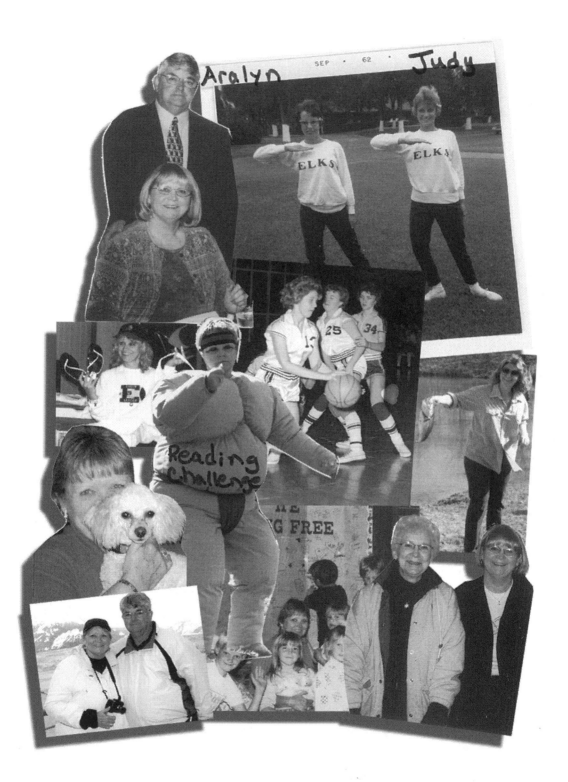

Aralyn SEP 62 Judy

ELKS ELKS

Reading Challenge

MARRIED, WITH CRITTERS

by Judy Johnson Ballard

My best friend growing up in a small community in western Oklahoma was Aralyn, the editor of this book. We did everything together. But during our senior year, for some reason, we got miffed at each other and went our separate ways. We did not speak for almost forty-nine years. Recently we reconnected, and she told me about this book. How interesting, we thought, that neither of us had chosen to have children.

As a child, my goal was to marry a rich man and have a baby girl and boy—the perfect family, the perfect life. More importantly, I remember wishing I were a boy because they seemed to have more fun. I never played with dolls. I never even did any baby-sitting. I played basketball and was a good athlete. In high school, I could not understand why the boys practiced after school and the girls had to practice the period before lunch. That meant we had to go to lunch with wet hair and spit baths. I was also a cheerleader, but had an alternate to cheer for me when I played in a game. The thing that aggravated me was that neither the alternate nor the other cheerleaders were required to come for the girls' games. Seeing this as unfair, I began to complain. Even though I was unaware yet that the Feminist Movement had begun, I guess I was becoming a member by speaking my mind. But this was the '60s—and I soon learned there were consequences for being an outspoken female. I was called to the principal's office and reprimanded for causing problems. Then at the end of the year, unlike all the years before, I did not receive an Honor Society award.

During that time, I began noticing that not every woman was treated equally. I was a naïve, middle-class white girl who was not aware of the world outside my little community. One of my best friends was also on the basketball team. She was a gifted player—and she was black. In my senior year, we went to the State Finals in Oklahoma City. I was shocked to hear our coach tell my dad that he had to call several motels before he found one that would allow blacks to stay. We had two on our team. While we were away for the tournament, we ate at a cafeteria. I thought nothing of sitting with my friend, but to this day I remember the rude comments and dirty looks other customers gave us. I realized then the added discrimination my friend had to endure every day. Looking back, I find it interesting, though, that I did not think one way or the other about the fact that my friend lived in a different part of town.

My choices when I graduated from high school were to either get married and have children or go to college. I chose the latter and went to Oklahoma State University. But with no idea of what I might study in preparation for a career, I wasn't sure why I was going. I suspect my goal was to get my "MRS." degree. At freshman orientation, one of the forms had a line on which we were to specify our major. I remember raising my hand and asking the proctor what I should put. He explained I was to fill in the blank with what I wanted to study. I was stunned that even before classes had begun I was expected to choose. Why hadn't someone told me what to study! Feeling pressured to finish the thing, I made a quick assessment. I'd made a B in my high school shorthand class, so being a secretary didn't seem feasible, and puke made me gag, which knocked out nursing. That left only one other possibility: I was going to be a teacher.

My parents had married when they were very young and Mother was just eighteen when I was born. She'd wanted other children, but they never happened. She told me repeatedly that whatever I did, don't get married young. I had to promise her I wouldn't marry before I was twenty-one. She and my father had grown up during the Dust Bowl, and they both worked hard for everything they had. Because my mom had a job outside the home, she was my role model for working hard if I wanted to succeed. She was a great cook, but she never taught me to cook. The only thing I remember about my time in the kitchen was being allowed to lick the pan after she'd made coconut cream pie.

I kept my promise to my mother and married my first husband two months after my twenty-first birthday. He wanted children right away, but I said no. I could barely take care of myself, much less a child. When my sister-in-law left her children with us for a week, two boys who were six and eight and her daughter who was one, I became convinced that I did not want to be a mom. If I were, I probably would have been arrested for child abuse. Everyone says it is different when they are your own. Maybe so, maybe not. I have to admit I like my dogs more than other people's dogs.

Besides just feeling ill-suited for motherhood, another reason I didn't want children was that every new mom I knew felt she needed to tell me how much pain she'd gone through during childbirth. So any time I had strong gas pains, the first thought I had was, "I never want to have children." As I matured I found my aversion to having a child had begun to lessen. Unfortunately, this awakening oc-

"...my life has been anything but barren... I have loved and been loved by hundreds of children throughout my career."

curred around the time I learned my husband was into other women. Going through divorce was the most emotionally painful experience of my life. Pain in childbirth, pain in divorce -- I was grateful not to have a child. All my energy went into simply surviving. I came out of the trauma a stronger woman, certain that I would never again allow a man to determine my fate.

I met my present husband when we were both thirty-nine, and I could hear the ticking of my biological clock. Now that I wanted to get pregnant, my husband went so far as to have his vasectomy reversed. I decided to see a fertility doctor who put the sperm directly into my cervix. On the way home I had a small amount of cramping, unlike any I'd had before, and was terrified I was already pregnant. I wasn't, but my reaction made me question whether I really wanted a child. We never tried the procedure again and I never got pregnant.

Though I'm childless, I can't imagine my life being more fulfilling. I've spent my forty-four years as an educator dedicated to helping children and as a speech-language pathologist, a counselor, and an administrator. I think often of a little boy who habitually picked at his forehead to the point of bleeding. As his counselor, I promised him that if he stopped he could come to my ranch and ride one of my horses. To my amazement, he did stop. After his head was completely healed, he came to my home and rode a horse, the first of many times that year. Watching his joy, I beamed with pride at what he had accomplished. And once when I was working as a speech-language pathologist, I was asked to give private therapy to a little girl who had never been able to swallow. When she finally learned how to drink from a straw, her mother and I both cried.

I've had many successes with children, and some failures. Sally, a sixth-grade girl who'd been a ward of the state as an infant and later adopted as a toddler, was having such serious problems with her adoptive parents that they wanted to negate the adoption. Working with her at school as her counselor, she and I became great friends. I decided to go through the labyrinth of procedures required to become a foster parent. I was going to save her! But once I was her foster parent, things changed. Sally wanted us to remain friends and resented my new role as mom. And honestly, I wasn't thrilled having all the responsibility that comes with taking care of a teenager. Sally ran away. When found, she again became a ward of the state. Years later she came to my home and thanked me for trying. I apologized for not having done a better job. She hadn't been ready to accept my help as a parent any more than I had been ready to be one.

Do I miss not having children? I think perhaps only at Christmas. I love the fantasy of having a big family come to our house and watching grandchildren open presents. The reality, though, I am not so sure of. This Norman Rockwell picture that fills my head every year tends to fade the day after Christmas.

I could never imagine living without animals. I have horses, cattle, dogs, goats, and a sheep that somehow found its way to our house. I've raised stray dogs, ducks, cats, and birds. My husband has always kept horses and cattle. When we met, our mutual love for animals was one of the things that drew us together. I'll admit to liking horses and dogs more than I like most people.

I've helped birth colts, calves, and dogs, then raised them on a bottle. These animals were my babies. The foal I'm now raising is a filly born April tenth. Her mother died of a snake bite twelve days later. I've fed the young horse twice a day ever since. She now nibbles on my neck and my hair (I think she's looking for a tit, but can't find one). Her name is Little Jude.

Some women tell me I was smart not to have children. Others tell me my decision shows I'm selfish and spoiled. One or two others have had the audacity to say, "You poor barren woman." To all of them I say this: I did what was right for me, and my life has been anything but barren. I have loved and been loved by hundreds of children throughout my career, and I treasure my animals. For the record, studies have shown that people without children are every bit as happy as people with them.

I am fortunate to have chosen the rewarding career I did. I've made a difference in many children's lives. But at the end of the day, I go home to my loving husband and our animals and a quiet house, where I am free to do whatever I want. While none of us should look back with regret at the choices we made in life, a few people I know have gone so far as to say they wouldn't change a thing.

Well, I suppose I can name a few things I'd change, such as losing my best friend in high school over something neither of us can remember. But my decision about having a child? That one never even made the Top Ten list.

Still having fun after forty-four years as an educator, Judy's adventures include traveling, enjoying time on her houseboat, fishing with her husband and mother (still going strong at age 85), learning to scuba dive - and, as always, taking care of her critters.

Images

April 29, The Daily Texan
Weekly Arts and Entertainment Magazine

Austin's actors on stage and off

BORDEN STERNBERG

Best Comedy - 2012
CAMP KICKITOO

MRS. RICHARD JAY BORDEN
Former TexAnn Freeman

'If I Dressed As Mother..'

BABY DERBY WINNER, 1947 MODEL
TexAnn Freeman graciously posed with a clay stork Sunday at the hospital show at the Dallas Health Museum. She is the daughter of Mr. and Mrs. Tanner H. Freeman Jr., 3608 Bellaire. She won last year's Dallas Baby Derby by being the first hospital baby born May 12, National Hospital Day. She won prizes worth about $800, including free hospital care and merchandise gifts. This year's Baby Derby will begin at one second after Tuesday midnight, with a similar pay-off awaiting the winner.

SPINNING THE GLOBE

by Annie Borden

Try as we might, we can't escape our generations.

I watched my mother, Mary Jo, chafe at the restrictions forced on a 1950s housewife and mother. She did what she needed to do to fulfill her roles, but something spurred her to bust out of unspoken constraints. My father always worked. He never made time for family vacations but my mother didn't let that stop her. Saving a little here and a little there from the grocery allowance, she'd set aside enough money by the end of the school year for us to do something fun. Into the car we three kids piled, Mom at the wheel, cigarette dangling from her lips, Corpus Christi in the rear-view. Up to San Antonio where we grabbed our funny, cool Grandma Zoe. Then northwest, heading for the Tetons or Colorado or New Mexico.

We camped, sleeping in tents, cooking over campfires, hiking trails . . . everything gave us a Mother Nature high. No one else's mom would consider even a day of camping, much less do it without a man. Our mom did it without blinking. Between camping trips, Mom kept our enthusiasm for adventure primed, spinning the globe and letting a finger land on some exotic travel possibility. My mother was a wonderful role model.

She did send mixed messages. While Mary Jo was raised a Southern Baptist and was well indoctrinated in those mores, she dreamed of roads never dared taken, like being a Las Vegas showgirl or a bartender somewhere. Despite these intimations of other life choices, she made it clear to me that I was to be a good girl, make good grades, go to college, and be chaste. At the same time, she said she thought I had a figure like Marilyn Monroe. I didn't. And wasn't Beau Geste a great read?

It was.

When Oswald's bullet shattered the country's innocence in November 1963, my family was already broken. One month earlier, grim-faced, our mother had gathered us around the kitchen table and announced that our father wanted a divorce. Brave and fun-loving no more, Mary Jo transformed before our eyes. It wasn't a comforting sight. Angry, fearful, weepy, crazed, pounds melting off her skinny body, she was a mess. We kids weren't much better. We all lost our bearings. What we thought was certain wasn't.

"For the first time in my life, no structure, no school, family, husband, or reputation can constrain me. I indulge in the sexual revolution, adding to my personal sociology research. Birth control pills preclude babies—pretty nifty."

People just didn't get divorced back then. Feeling like social pariahs, we pack everything in a moving van, say goodbye to life-long friends, and drive up to Austin where Mom's folks live. Two months later, our father marries a woman the same age as Mom with three kids of her own. We are replaced. It hurts—a lot.

Mary Jo, desperate, scrambles and finds a teaching job to support her three teenagers. Most afternoons after school, she teaches piano to neighbor kids and at night she attends graduate school at the University of Texas. Exhausted and frightened, she has little time to monitor, praise, or even chastise my brother, sister, and me.

At seventeen and over the next few years, I learn two big lessons that deeply affect my life. First lesson: Marriage does not necessarily last. A man can't be counted on to stay, provide financial support, and help raise the kids. Matrimony is a suspect goal and men's reliability questionable.

With the '60s in full-throttle, I evolve into a radical, atheistic hippie, rejecting my conservative upbringing. My brother quits high school and joins the Marines to fight in Vietnam; my little sister goes a bit off the rails, unsupervised by my now very busy mom. Second lesson: Kids can cast you aside to live a life that frightens, upsets, shames, embarrasses you. The struggles of motherhood look like a raw deal.

Soon after our move to Austin, I start dating a university student from New York. I graduate from high school, register for my first semester in art school at UT, and have sex for the first time—all within twenty-four hours. What's more, I have broken an important rule: you must be a virgin for your husband! Several years go by, and I solve that problem with a marriage license. We marry to get my mom off my back. Living out of wedlock is still verboten in 1967. Pregnancy is no longer a fear because, as a married woman, I can get those wonderful new birth control pills at the student health clinic.

My husband, Rich, and I finish our degrees at UT and head to Kent State for graduate school. Here we encounter political and social radicals, couples interested in wife swapping (not me, too prudish) and professors who make indelicate passes. It is 1968 and the sexual revolution has sprung up right there alongside Students for a Democratic Society and the Black Panther Party. Stability is the least of our concerns; anything is possible. Having a baby never crosses our minds. My husband, busy with his experimental psych research, takes on a sexy undergraduate research assistant who phones him daily. Attraction is in the air. I know where this is going, and I'm not going to be there when it happens. I will not become my mother and I will not crumble!

We consider going to New York for the Woodstock Festival but the tickets are too expensive. Instead we travel to San Francisco where I plan to stay, advanced degree in sociology be damned. Rich goes back to Kent State to finish his master's degree and our lives diverge. If we knew then that everyone got into Woodstock for free, we would have gone there, and this story would be different.

Once Rich leaves, I'm free at last. For the first time in my life, no structure, no school, family, husband, or reputation can constrain me. I indulge in the sexual revolution, adding to my personal sociology research. Birth control pills preclude babies—pretty nifty.

I'm able to save some money, $440 to be exact. Rich wants me to spend it on a divorce. Forget it! Not about to miss an opportunity to travel, I spend it instead on a one-way ticket to Europe.

Having several weeks before my overseas plane departs, I go to San Francisco. One day while I am selling underground newspapers on the corner in Berkeley, I get word that something has happened back at Kent State. It isn't clear what, but in time it is all over the news: shortly after noon Eastern Time, the Ohio National Guard shot and killed students who'd gathered on the campus mall to protest Nixon's escalation of the war. Rich is there! Frantically, I try him by phone but all the lines are jammed. It takes me three days to finally get through. He had been there when the shots were fired, standing right next to a woman whose head was blown off. That could have been me. He's shaken and doesn't want to relive the experience. I am relieved he is alive, but now I can't leave this crazy country soon enough.

Hope replaces horror as I hitchhike from one country to another. Happy globe-spinning memories become reality. I live outside the States for three years, from May 1970 to March 1973. When crossing borders, I am asked if I am "Miss" or "Mrs." My glib reply is, "Take your pick . . . either one!" I am in my element. Fantasies and desires from childhood come to life: islands in Greece; sailing the Mediterranean; traveling overland to India and back; living in a garret and performing in the theater in Paris.

My wandering life comes to a close with a letter from Mom. My baby sister is having a baby, solo. With airfare from my mother, I come home to be a part of the child's life. Raymond's birth relieves me of pressure to produce grandchildren for Mom and gives me the opportunity to be significant in a young person's life. I bond deeply with him. Once again, no reliable man is in the picture.

Years pass and Mary Jo never remarries, becoming bitter and set in her ways. Although I have many boyfriends, I don't settle down either and begin to notice I'm getting set in my ways, too. The single life is less and less appealing or satisfying and I feel the need to have a family, but not a baby—not alone—no way, no how! As life would have it, at age thirty-five, I meet a man who already has a child. Ric is the man and his son is Reed, then a fifteen-year-old boy, whose mother left when he was eighteen months old. Ric had raised his son, however haphazardly, throughout the craziness of the late '60s and '70s. Ah ha! Here is a man I can trust, a man who is clearly capable of sticking around and loving someone even when it is hard. I let down my guard and begin a new, cooperative adventure in which flexibility is essential, particularly as it involves living with a teenage boy.

For the first time in my life, I consider having a baby because I know Ric will stay and be a good dad. But he, after so many years as a single parent, has absolutely no interest in starting a new family. I know that if I become pregnant, I will be tempted to have the baby, so I hope I don't. It is a choice I do not want to be forced to make. A year later, the problem becomes moot. I develop a pelvic inflammatory disease, resulting in a complete hysterectomy. Funny, despite the trauma of that experience, I am relieved that the question of my having a child is no longer in my hands.

Time passes. Reed grows into a man, marries, and has two kids. Because his own mom had abandoned him as a baby, she is out of the picture. I am there from the beginning. I am it! The cool grandma, like Grandma Zoe.

It is what I wanted all along. And to this day, I am amazed at my good fortune.

A five-year breast cancer survivor, Annie is a Professor of 3D Modeling at the Game Development Institute in Austin, Texas. She served as Associate Producer on Camp Kickitoo, a feature film in distribution in Africa. She travels, practices Kundalini Yoga and paints in her studio by the Pedernales River, where she and her husband live in their strawbale house.

QUESTION AUTHORITY

by Kathleen Clark

When first I saw that iconic motto QUESTION AUTHORITY, I had to ask what it meant! In the world I grew up in, that was not allowed.

Parented by uneducated, hard-drinking, Polish-Catholic, second-generation immigrants, I grew up in Grand Prairie, Texas, a town of 30,000 sandwiched between Dallas and Fort Worth. My family was isolated by choice, trusting no one and having no friends in this WASP-y, middle-class town.

At home, my volatile mother ruled the family and provided day care for more than thirty children by wielding her giant, red plastic bat. Having been traumatized by her father, the crazy town drunk, she was the least likely candidate for nurturing or providing mothering. No one dared challenge her—even as she beat my six-day-old younger brother, a scene that has never left my mind. Myself a bruised and beaten six-year-old watching this, and with no adult having ever dared to intervene when my mother lashed out, my only hope had been to pray nightly that she would die. Being motherless seemed preferable.

Added to this was my education in a Roman Catholic school, where disobedience had perverse punishments such as kneeling in front of the class, arms outstretched, hands palm-up and burdened by heavy books. Switched on my legs by Sister Josephine in first grade for talking aloud, I never disobeyed again.

Obeying rules served me well. Academically talented, I was the first in my extended family to attend college. Socially, I was shy and awkward, clinging to rules for guidance. I spent much time in "the stacks," ponderous accumulations of library books amassed over decades at The University of Texas in Austin.

Freshman year, autumn 1964, my roommate introduced me to a student, Richard, three years older than I. Stable and agreeable, Richard was tolerant of those who were not. One of his friends was Charles Whitman, the notorious 1966 UT Tower Sniper. Richard laughed off Charlie's intense, silent rages as "just Charlie." Most who knew Charlie could hear the ticking bomb. When it exploded on that fateful August day, I was spending the summer break at my parents' home. Seeing Charlie's photo flashed across the TV screen, I called Richard. He was mildly surprised and fairly dismissive of the horror. I would later realize that Richard kept strong emotions at a distance. Having a shy, soft-spoken girlfriend such as I was easy for him. Having a detached yet kind boyfriend was all I needed.

Dry humping was our most extreme intimacy during our three years of dating. Birth control pills were elusive in 1965. A girl claiming menstrual irregularity might be given a temporary prescription from the UT Student Health Center, but outside UT, a single woman risked humiliation for daring to seek sex without exposure to pregnancy. My own roommate was physically chased from a doctor's office. Richard and I were virgins when we wed. Abortions were illegal. People still counted the months after a couple married before the birth of a child.

Two months after we wed in 1968, Richard, having graduated, lost his draft-deferred status and left for basic training and the Vietnam War. This postponed the conception of my babies Jeffrey and Cecily, names chosen even before we wed, as I was certain I would be a mother.

Richard's friends encouraged me to live with my parents. Instead, I attended social work graduate school on a National Institute of Mental Health grant, arranged for me by a professor impressed by my Phi Beta Kappa status. Not returning home was my first act of independence.

In Waiting Wives, a national support group for military spouses, I sought refuge but found no connection. Dropping out, I began marching in war protests and roaming with masses of dissenters, shouting, "HELL NO! WE WON'T GO!"

Meanwhile, Richard and I exchanged cassette tapes via military mail. Learning to sing Leonard Cohen's "Hey, That's No Way To Say Goodbye," I sent my rendition to him. During the next two years, I saw Richard twice, for six days each time, dutifully staying in a bedroom next to his parents, a small ventilation fan fitted into the wall, inhibiting physical privacy. We delayed Jeffrey and Cecily by using the now widely popular birth control pills.

Unscathed mentally or physically, Richard returned to Austin. He worked at a state agency and settled in with his manly hobbies: hunting, building canoes, refurbishing abandoned cars, watching football on TV. He designed and built our house. Serving as a children's mental health therapist in an agency, I had only my professional identity. Depressed, I consulted my family doctor, who advised me to have a baby. When I told Richard this he replied, not unkindly, "We already have a baby…YOU!" I was prepared to fulfill my role as a woman by becoming a mother, but he had a profound understanding of my emotional immaturity. Trained to be obedient and have no opinions of my own, I did as he wished. Faithfully I took birth control pills, often wondering why since we had sex at most once monthly.

With no signs of unhappiness emanating from Richard, I was blindsided when, seven years later, he divorced me, marrying a mother of two preschoolers. As frightened as an abandoned child, I was left with no guidance. I was the first person in all my extended family to be divorced as well as excommunicated from the Catholic Church, to which I had forced Richard to convert for our marriage.

Once again, I was breaking new ground: I knew no wife who had ever been divorced. I had no female friends. My sole activity being work, it was there I discovered the perfect lover for someone coming out of a sex-starved marriage. Brian was handsome, narcissistic, well-endowed, and, of course, alcoholic—part of my family-of-origin's life-pattern curse. Many marvelous hour-upon-hour "lunches" were spent making love. Sleep was impossible when I lay next to this male. I longed to carry his baby inside me, to hold a tiny him-me in my arms.

On a road trip with Brian from Austin to Houston, I awakened from my pheromone-driven intoxication. A man who could drink a case of beer while driving those 147 miles would not be a good husband or father. Six years passed before I set myself free from him, much of it spent with my own psychotherapist, a surrogate womb for my undeveloped being shrouded in an adult body. When I spoke to her of my masochistic sexual fantasies one day, she pointed out, "Brian IS a masochistic fantasy!" Licking my nipples in the early afternoon, he had often declared "no sex tonight", baffling and tormenting me. This passionate love affair had been only a variation on my subjugation to authority.

"Faithfully I took birth control pills, often wondering why since we had sex at most once monthly... I was blindsided when, seven years later, he divorced me, marrying a mother of two preschoolers."

Unbound, I slowly created a new life. I developed relationships with single women and ventured into new activities, such as aerobic dancing, happy-hours, and teaching Sunday school at the Unity Church.

When a co-worker broke up with her abrasive boyfriend, Max, he asked me out. Ignoring my intuitive response, I fell back into obedience. Saying "no" was unimaginable when a possibility for a romantic relationship popped up. Much about him suggested that Max—an elementary school teacher—was a good man. He was responsible and financially stable and not a heavy drinker. A year after our first date, we discussed marriage. Why pay two rents?

Once we were married, I discovered Max's moodiness and quick temper. Fearful of his fury, I could never be on the phone when he arrived home. His face contorted into a peanut-shape, reddened, ears steaming. For Jeffrey and Cecily I decided "never this fear!" I was relieved when Max insisted we have no children, his decision being related to retinitis pigmentosa, a genetically linked progressive blindness.

Max wanted me home more, insisting I quit the agency and begin a private practice or be divorced. Cringing, I quit my job of fifteen years. Building my business took longer than he wanted, so he ranted about women taking advantage of men. Yet he fled from emotional intimacy with me, developing an obsession with marathon running. The dutifully supportive wife, I attended all the races. Bored and sexually dead with each other, weekends of mutual margaritas aided Max and me when we were alone.

Part of me was drying up. Menopause was my conjecture, but my male doctor refused to provide a simple hormone blood test, insisting I was too young at forty. Despite the loss of many female characteristics—no luscious butt, shrinking breasts, a vagina almost impenetrable—I still listened to authority, suffering obediently rather than speaking up for my own body.

After seven years Max divorced me to marry a nine-year-old's mother twenty years younger than I. At forty-five, I was partially frozen in time, still an emotionally motherless child, bewildered about my fate.

Unexpectedly, my familial female curse, ovarian cancer, appeared. I chose a female ob-gyn as my guide. A total hysterectomy led me to cancer-free status. In denial throughout my entire menopause, I now realized Jeffrey and Cecily would never exist. My darlings, a war delayed you, an emotionally fragile mother I spared you, an alcoholic or angry father would not be yours. Your names, chosen in my youth, would never be forgotten. I could refocus now, searching for a lasting relationship with a man just for myself.

I gave myself the authority to set my own course of action. To my gal-pals' horror, I used a free local newspaper with personal ads to find dating opportunities. I kept a book of ad clippings and assessments of the men's voice mail box messages, jotting down my feelings after being in their presence. I met many guys, some intriguing, some lackluster—all of whom I would never have otherwise encountered. It was fun!

Responding to an unremarkable ad two years later, I was irked that the man sounded young and gay. However, I left my phone number anyway as a brusque reply. Meeting this man at a jazz club, his physical appearance was of little appeal: short, hooked nose, slight build. Blazing sapphire-blue eyes and thick, curly hair were his only apparent assets. Ron, who owned a janitorial supply store, called himself a "toilet paper magnate." Unexpectedly, his degree was in psychology.

Synchronicities astonished us: our mutual dentist had tried to set us up on a blind date in the past few months; Ron's brother had been appointed to

Texas State Board of Psychologists, replacing an ex-lover of mine; Ron and I recalled briefly meeting decades earlier at an opening for a shop next to his business.

Ron was the most incredibly nurturing man I had ever met. I continually discovered sweet, intuitive aspects of his nature. This was a male? Physically, his touch became increasingly thrilling and calming, simultaneously. I had never been so well-treated. I had never known what love truly was until this relationship with a man most females had chosen not to date. He was a diamond left lying in the midst of gravel.

Insisting we date seven years (the length of each of my marriages), I wed Ron at the Elvis Chapel in Las Vegas 2001. We felt we had won the lottery of love, worth far more than money!

Years later in a therapy session, a ten-year-old client asked, "Can I see what's inside that locket around your neck?" I hesitated: therein was a photo of Ron on our first Halloween together. I had dressed him as an old woman: cotton house coat, I-Love-Lucy-scarfed head, drooping knee-high stockings, gaudy earrings, old-fashioned make-up on his face. I opened the locket.

"Is that your mother?" she asked.

I smiled with tender serenity, "Yes."

Kathleen is living happily ever after, faithful to her mottos:

OLD ENOUGH TO KNOW BETTER, YOUNG ENOUGH TO DO IT ANYWAY!

And: TOO MUCH GOOD TASTE IS BORING!

~ 1967 ~

Fire aboard Apollo 1 kills all 3 astronauts
First Be-In: Golden Gate Park, CA
Central Park Be-In: 10,000 attend
Six-Day War: Israel takes West Bank
Supreme Court rules interracial marriage constitutional
Thurgood Marshall: first black Supreme Court justice
Race riots/anti-war riots sweep the US
First pop festival: Monterey, CA
Hair opens off-Broadway
John McCain shot down, taken prisoner in Vietnam
Crowned: *The Shah of Iran*
Debut: *Rolling Stone Magazine*
First Super Bowl
First ATM – UK
First human heart transplant

Married: *Elvis and Priscilla*
Songs: *Sgt. Pepper's Lonely Hearts Club Band*

Movies: *Dirty Dozen; Guess Who's Coming to Dinner;*
In the Heat of the Night

Born: *Tim McGraw/Faith Hill; Nicole Kidman/Keith*
Urban; Will Ferrell; Harry Connick, Jr; Kate Walsh;
Julia Roberts

Deaths: *Otis Redding, age 26; Jayne Mansfield, age 34*

Story sent to Mom in hospital when Jay was born.   April 1961

Midnight

Midnight wa
hor

MEDINA HIGH SCHOOL ANNUALS have arrived
first carton of the yearbooks are Carol Bilicsky (r)
Eddy, a staff member. Graduates of the 1968-69 c

4 Another horse (race)   2. ½ mile

a two furlongs 40.40,
e, that'd be keen!" said
r him!"

THE BIG DECISION THAT WASN'T

by Melissa J. Eddy

The only thing missing was the white picket fence; otherwise my idyllic childhood was complete. Growing up in small-town Ohio, I was the eldest child of college-educated parents whose marriage was solid. Dad worked and mom made our home. Money was tight, but my two younger brothers and I never lacked anything of importance. I doted on my siblings and squabbled with them. All of us were encouraged by our parents to be independent, and, like most kids back then, we were allowed to roam, often bicycling from one end of town to the other. Such freedom in my early life set the stage for what was to come: an adventurous, resilient adulthood. What this oh-so-traditional picture did not include was a bevy of cuddly baby dolls; my penchant for active independence as a child clashed with any notions of motherhood as an adult.

Of course I had dolls—I just wasn't emotionally attached to them the way other girls were. I played infrequently and only perfunctorily with Betsy Wetsy ("Give her a real bottle and she wets!"). Later I was given a Barbie, who spent most of her time in a dresser drawer. I much preferred kicking a ball around with the neighborhood boys, swimming at the community pool, or playing with my collection of horse figurines. I had a passion for horses: read books about them, spent endless hours drawing them, and fervently wished for one of my own. When I was nine, I wrote a story as a gift for my mother, who was in the hospital after giving birth to my youngest brother. It wasn't about a baby—it was about a horse. After Mom and baby brother came home, I helped care for him and babysat him and other infants in the neighborhood, but children who could walk and talk were more to my liking. Babies just didn't interest me, so having one never crossed my mind.

In my preteen years, horses gave way to boys and the Beatles. Playing my Beatles records until their grooves were worn, I dreamed of that magical moment when some boy I had a crush on would want to hold my hand. Alas, that didn't happen for a long time because none of them had a crush on me. Many of my friends were boys, but I didn't have a boyfriend, or even a date, until my senior year when a boy from church asked me out. It didn't matter that Paul was a year younger and inches shorter—this was a date! On our second outing we did hold hands and over time engaged in a fair amount of making out, but nothing more; we were "good kids." We went steady until I graduated, then amicably broke up before I left for college, more than two hundred miles away. Neither of us wanted to be tied to a long-distance relationship.

Realizing, in my late-teen wisdom, how colossally boring my little town was, I could hardly wait to leave, to experience the world. For that I chose to go as far away as my mother would allow: Michigan. The small college I attended had a study-abroad program and was in a city ten times the size of my hometown; I felt so urbane. I soaked up all the deep, late-night conversations, discovered psychology, and immersed myself in studies that, for the first time, were truly demanding. Included in my new circle of friends were boys on the verge of becoming men. After a few casual dates and brief crushes, a deeper relationship blossomed. His name was Mark, and I fell in love. Our physical attraction was strong, but we never went all the way. I held back, perhaps sensing his level of commitment was not as deep as mine. Sure enough, a few months before I departed to study abroad, he abruptly broke up with me.

I was crushed. Looking for books to help me understand and heal, I scoured the college library. It was there that I discovered feminism. I had never seen myself as oppressed or had given little thought to traditional gender roles, so reading Betty Friedan and Simone de Beauvoir was a revelation. I quickly became enlightened as I devoured book after book by and about powerful women. When the time came for me to board my first transatlantic flight to spend six months in Germany, I felt, once again, strong and independent.

By then I also had met the man who was to become my first husband. His name was George, a transfer student who, at six feet ten inches tall, was hard to miss. My first impression was far from positive—I found him unattractive and socially awkward. He asked me out; I turned him down. While overseas, I didn't give him a second thought. The wealth of experiences I had in Europe swept me into adulthood, from hours of introspective journaling to struggling with university classes in German, from pub-crawling to visiting the Continent's great cities. In a single weekend I fell in and out of love with a man I'd met on a tour to Prague. In Provence I had a romantic interlude with a college classmate who was studying there. And I remained a virgin.

Back on my Michigan campus, George asked me out again. I had to admit he did have certain attractions: he had an apartment and a car. Also, I was dazzled by his musical talent and ambition. While several of my female friends were sporting engagement rings, in truth, no one else was even asking me out, so I accepted. Soon I was drawn into his dark intensity and his passion for music. Our relationship bloomed and after a few months we were engaged.

"When Mother Nature was passing out maternal instinct, I had stepped out of line to go to the bathroom."

Certain of his commitment and finally ready for sex, I made an appointment with Planned Parenthood and started on The Pill. I wanted to make love, but, looking toward graduate school the next year, I emphatically did not want to make a baby. We married the summer after I graduated, and while I worked on my master's degree to become a counselor, George completed his bachelor's degree. By then it was clear he had no future as a professional musician, and his bitter disillusionment put an early strain on our relationship.

In our third year of marriage, we tired of the cold Michigan winters and moved to Austin, Texas, where I took a counseling job at the newly founded

shelter for battered women. I was excited being at the cutting edge of a movement that was saving women's lives. George was bored, working as a bank
teller. With increasingly little in common, the relationship unraveled. Both in-
troverts, we struggled to find something to talk about; car trips went by in excruciating silence. He started spending late nights out and I didn't ask where.

I knew in my heart the marriage couldn't last, but I didn't have the nerve
to say so. Yet, inexplicably, for the first time in my life, I began to think about
having a baby. Many friends were starting their families. Was it time for me,
too? I was ambivalent. I had never felt a reproductive drive and still didn't, and
I knew having a baby was not the way to save a marriage. But my pregnant
friends glowed with happiness, and I wondered if I was missing something.

I began to be distressed about George's late nights away, and one evening
I told him if he went out that night, he would find the chain on the door
when he came home. He went anyway, and when I confronted him later, he
confessed he'd been having an affair. Furious, I insisted he move out immediately. I cried hard, crumpled on the kitchen floor, and called my parents to
tell them of the separation. But in a matter of days, my anger and hurt turned
to relief, and a few weeks later, after a brief, unsuccessful attempt at marriage
counseling, I filed for divorce. I was grateful I had not acted on that fleeting
maternal impulse. A child would have complicated the break-up and forced
me to remain in contact with him for years to come.

Single again for less than a year, I met the man who would become my
second—and forever—husband. I wasn't looking, even though I had thought
a lot about what I did and did not want in a man. And I had made peace with
the possibility that I might remain permanently alone. Then I met Tracy. It
was, for him, love at first sight, and my feelings quickly followed. He was
easy to talk to, confident, and passionate about his work, i.e., different from
George in every important way. Tracy had two young daughters from his first
marriage, and I became very fond of them. We both knew what we wanted:
each other.

There was just one potential problem: while still married to his first wife,
Tracy had decided two children were enough and gotten a vasectomy. He told
me about the surgery early in our relationship, in casual conversation, where-
upon I happily took myself off The Pill. But when the conversation turned to
marriage, he sat me down one evening, looked me in the eye, and repeated:

He could not father any more children. He asked if that mattered to me.

The decision I had to make was one that would affect me for the rest of my life. Did I want to bear children, or did I want him? He told me to think about it for as long as I needed to.

It took me about ten seconds: I wanted him. In that moment the reality crystallized that physically having a baby had never been important to me and what little maternal instinct I possessed could be expressed by nurturing his daughters. Yes, I wanted him.

I have never regretted that decision. While our marriage of thirty-plus years has had its ups and downs and we differ in many ways, our love and partnership are solid. Without full-time childrearing responsibilities, I have been able to pursue demanding professional work in several fields, volunteering widely, following my passion for choral performance, and traveling. I loved helping raise his daughters, who were three and six when we married; part-time parenting suited me well. Much like being a grandparent, I cared for them and played with them when they were with us, then sent them home to their full-time parent and resumed my own life. My stepdaughters are grown now with families of their own, and I remain close to them and enjoy the eight grandchildren whom I consider as much mine as his. My life is full.

Sometimes I still wonder what made the big decision so easy. Was it because I was loath to give up my independence in the service of motherhood? Possibly. Did I have some kind of hormonal deficit? Could be. Or maybe it's just that when Mother Nature was passing out maternal instinct, I had stepped out of line to go to the bathroom.

Now a writer/editor after stints as a psychotherapist and nonprofit executive, Melissa lives in the Texas Hill Country with her husband and pets. She sings with two choirs, spends time with her family, serves as board president of two nonprofits and travels whenever possible. She has little spare time, which is fine with her.

Massage
Publications

Peggy Lamb formed Moving Collaborations in 19__

Someone's got to lead

By Melissa Morrison
Staff Writer of The Dallas Morning News

Enterprising women give choreographers chance to step out

Peggy Lamb and Karen Bower Robinson, their faces and bodies covered with flowing fabric, sway and twist like phantoms. They're rehearsing a dance piece dubbed "The Shroud" in a classroom-cum-rehearsal hall decorated with children's construction-paper artwork and cartoon characters. Their accompaniment is a haunting composition by Tangerine Dream — and the sounds of a ping-pong tournament across the hall at Dan's Recreation Center.

The piece will be part of *Memories*, a showcase of __ choreographers' work. It

dancer in Dallas.

When dancer Gene Connor arrives for a rehearsal, Ms. __ half-jokingly gives him a handful of fliers and urges him to distribute them to the pingpong __ and Mary Kay Cosmetics __ sentatives gathered in neighboring rooms.

This is Moving Collaborations' third showcase since the first in 1988. (There wasn't one in 1989, because they couldn't afford it, Ms. Lamb says.) "Every year we learn a bit more," Ms. Lamb says.

For this production, the Bathhouse Cultural Center has donated a performance space __ designer — as __ fliers for free.

Wild Sober Woman

DANCING MY OWN DANCE

by Peggy Lamb

I never questioned my decision not to have children until the past couple of years. As I watch family and friends glow with happiness when they talk about their grandchildren, a deep yearning springs from within me—unbidden and unwanted. These are the times I long for an extended family, surrounded by children and grandchildren who share my genes, a legacy complete with bones and breath and unconditional love.

The urge to bear children just wasn't in me—quite the opposite, in fact. I often joked to friends that I was too narcissistic to have children. If I had a child who happened to be hungry, I'd say, "Here, have some peanuts," then return to what I was doing. While I'd never claim to be totally devoid of narcissism, the deeper truth is that my desires and goals simply never included children. I knew in my soul that without a serious longing to be a mother, my bringing a child into the world would be wrong for me, and certainly for the child.

For as long as I can remember, I have danced my own dance. Traditional marriage and children were not a good fit for me, especially when I was young and the drum beats I followed were orchestrated by my innate rebellious nature.

At the age of twenty-seven, having spent years in a shroud of despair and alcoholism, I finally broke free from my addiction, determined to embrace sobriety. When I was thirty, I married a fellow member of AA who already had a child and was unsure he wanted another. In the early years of our marriage, I lingered on the fence as to whether or not to have children. Then, during my mid-to-late thirties, with my biological clock ticking, I became more mature in my sobriety, recognizing ever more clearly who I really was. It was from this place of unwavering self-awareness that I made the deliberate decision to remain childless.

That decision was unquestionably the right one for me. Admittedly, I sometimes yearn to be part of a larger clan, but I treasure the dazzling array of rhythms my freedom has afforded me. My legacy resides within the hundreds of dances I've choreographed, the poems I've composed, the glass art I've created, my books for massage

"For as long as I can remember, I have danced my own dance."

therapists, as well as in my work with female prisoners and through thousands to whom I've taught massage therapy and dance.

But the deepest legacy for me, and the one of which I am most proud, is in the knowledge that I was always true to myself.

Teaching workshops around the country, traveling to Ireland to reconnect with her Irish roots, and dog-sledding in Minnesota feed Peggy's adventurous spirit. Her favorite days are those spent teaching creative movement to female prisoners. A native New Yorker, she lives in Austin, enjoying the wonders of the Southwest.

~ 1968 ~

*News worldwide: Hundreds of feminists protest at
Miss America Pageant
Av. yearly income: $7,800
Av. rent: $130/mo
Min. wage: $1.60/hr
Columbia U: student occupation makes US headlines
Martin Luther King; Bobby Kennedy assassinated
LBJ announces he won't run again
Pope bans The Pill for Catholics
First Boeing 747 flight
Apollo 8: first humans to orbit the moon
First US ATM machine, Philadelphia
First Big Mac: 49 cents
Richard Nixon elected president*

Married: *Jackie Kennedy and Aristotle Onassis*

New: *911 emergency service*
Invented: *Air bags*

TV debut: *60 Minutes (longest run in T.V. history)*

Movies: *The Graduate; Rosemary's Baby;
Bonnie and Clyde*

Tunes: *Hey Jude; Stoned Soul Picnic; MacArthur Park;
Dock of the Bay; Light My Fire*

I CAN SEE CLEARLY NOW

by Deby Bell

I've been a coward. Until I'd witnessed how the women contributors to this book have held nothing back, I refused to revisit one of the most secret and painful events of my life.

I had an abortion.

During my junior year at UT-Austin, I had casual, unprotected sex.

The result was not so casual. When I missed my period, I was pretty sure why.

Feeling stupid and ashamed, I didn't want even my once-a-year doctor to know, and certainly didn't want him to log the information in my medical records. Since home pregnancy tests didn't exist in 1970, I found a GYN to confirm my worst fear. A church near campus gave me the number of a clinic to call and schedule a legal abortion—not in Austin, but in Albuquerque. The cost for the procedure, a plane ticket and a motel room was going to be more than $300, which I did not have. A dear, sweet man, the landlord for my apartment, agreed to lend me the money. In turn, I agreed to pay him back $35 a month. It was easier for me to speak of my situation to him, an acquaintance, than to have told my brother. I needed my brother's support, but I knew he'd be disappointed in me. And why shouldn't he be? I was. So, he never knew.

I began the ordeal by driving to Dallas, flying from there to Albuquerque.

When I arrived, I checked into a motel near the clinic. I remember thinking, "Every single person in this motel knows why I'm here." Certainly the taxi driver who drove me early the next morning to the clinic knew. Inside I found other young women, all dressed in white gowns, glancing cautiously at one another in the waiting room. No one spoke. Each of us was given a sedative and sat there, waiting to be called. When it was my turn, I was led into a cold, overly lit surgery room. The mood was perfunctory, one of getting business done, which was fine by me. Hanging on the wall opposite me, as I lay on the table, was an oversized clock. I watched the minutes as they oh-so-slowly ticked by. When the procedure was over, I rested for a couple of hours in another room until the cramping was fairly contained. Then I flew back to Texas. I spent the next twenty-four hours on the couch of a friend. Within forty-eight hours, I was back on campus, sitting in a classroom as though nothing had changed.

My life appeared no different from that of most teenagers...I was unaware that beneath this 'normal' facade lay serious issues just waiting to surface."

But something had changed— I had changed. No longer feeling young and carefree, I even told one of my closest friends, "I can't" when she asked me to be her maid of honor. I didn't explain why. She cried, saying she didn't want a wedding if I wasn't going to be part of it. Unable to bear how deeply my refusal was hurting her, I relinquished, but to this day, I remember very little about her wedding.

Growing up in Killeen, adjacent to Fort Hood, life was different from life in nonmilitary towns. My friends and I were the "town kids" whose parents were in business. On payday weekends at the base, checks became cash, and cash was quickly spent. Cars with shiny wheels and loud stereos would crawl along Avenue D. Think American Graffiti minus the film's sense of innocence. This was the mid-'60s, the atmosphere rougher. Inside these cars were soldiers one step away from the jungles of Vietnam. They weren't just going to the malt shop; they were stopping on street corners and making deals with tall, dark women sporting short-shorts, high heels, wild wigs, and a whole lot of attitude. Providing us with a new source of entertainment, these seedy scenes became quite the hit with our out-of-town guests.

As Walter Cronkite was ending the evening news each night with the death count from Vietnam, my life appeared, by all accounts, no different from that of most teenagers. I went to Friday night football games and hung out at the Longhorn Drive-In, indulging in tater-tots and lots of flirting. I was unaware that beneath this "normal" facade lay serious issues just waiting to surface.

My parents were loving and successful and generous. But our lives changed dramatically when my father drank. I'd host slumber parties only when my parents were going to be out of town. Otherwise, if Dad was home, my friends might also experience Dad's slurring his words and stumbling, should that be one of his drinking nights. On dates, I dreaded the possibility we'd run into him, already homesteading at some restaurant's bar. There was never any physical abuse, just angry words and scenes so ugly they are tattooed on my brain. Even before getting pregnant, I'd made the decision not to have a baby. Recreating a "family" held no appeal for me and wasn't the road I planned to choose.

Instead of following the usual route toward marriage and children, I unconsciously, but actively, took steps assuring I would fail. "Deby, you sabotage every relationship you get into," a friend once told me. When dating someone, I would quickly announce I never intended to marry. Fearful of getting pregnant again, and not wanting to be on the pill for decades, I had a tubal ligation when I was twenty-six. This gave me peace of mind, but I was still unaware of why I was broken and unable to sustain healthy relationships.

Thanks to an *Oprah* show, I finally heard the term, ACA—Adult Child of an Alcoholic—when I was thirty-five. Unbeknownst to me until that time, virtually all the decisions I made and actions I took were rooted in the fact that I was an ACA.

But alcoholism is a disease. It is not the person. So, that same year, when my father quit drinking, our family was given a second chance. I've been able to forgive myself and my Dad. Memories now bring me smiles. And for that, I am forever grateful.

Deby believes "More is better: more choices, more time, more freedom and more independence." She is grateful for her family, friends and health. Her interests include glass art, seeing the natural beauty of our country and good wine. Why not!

"Women may be the one group that grows more radical with age."

Gloria Steinem

Recipient of the Presidential Medal of Freedom, 2013

~ 1969 ~

Neal Armstrong: first man on the moon
250,000 anti-war protestors march in DC
Golda Meir of Wisconsin elected Israeli PM
Woodstock: over 400,000 attend
Cat 5 Hurricane Camille hits Mississippi, 248 dead
Beatles: Last public performance

***TV debuts**: Sesame Street (US); Monty Python (UK)*

***Movies**: Midnight Cowboy: first X-rated film to win an
Oscar*
*Alice's Restaurant; Easy Rider; Butch Cassidy & the
Sundance Kid; They Shoot Horses, Don't They?*

***Tunes**: Sugar Sugar; Aquarius; Sweet Caroline; Lay Lady
Lay; Easy to be Hard; This Girl is a Woman Now; Suspicion;
Honky Tonk Women; Wedding Bell Blues;
The Worst that Could Happen*

James Taylor: first record deal

***Deaths:** Decade ends in violence:*
1 dead at Rolling Stones concert in Altamont, CA;

Acknowledgements

I am grateful to my friends, the writers of this book, who trusted me enough to join in this adventure. Their wisdom surpassed their egos such that each of them allowed herself to become vulnerable in order to share the truth of her story. I am especially indebted to two dedicated women in our group:

Jane Burkett, who read each draft of every story with a critical eye, offering valuable insight and constructive feedback with cleverness and wit. Jane's talent and workmanship were valuable contributions, paramount to the production of the book.

Mary-Ellen Campbell, who worked tirelessly and creatively on the book's formatting and the design of our graphics. A talented artist with a heart of gold and an abundance of patience, Mary-Ellen made pleasant those tasks which seemed overwhelming to many of us.

Thanks to our cheerleaders, Maggie Gallant and Pamela Gooby, themselves child-free women, but not yet sixty, thus too young to be contributors. Our proofreader, Howie Richey; Spider Johnson, Norman Witzler, Grace McEvoy, Elise Krentzel and Carol Provence.

Others to whom we owe thanks are Ann Caldwell, Christine Gilbert, Jeanne Stites Newell, Marianne Dorman, Vickie Cotrell, Suzanne Johnson, Deannie Rule, Elaine Eddins, Bonnie Drenik, Donna O'Klock, Phil Eagleton, Karen Kreps, Anne Markley and Martha Knock-Ward.

Thanks also to talented writer Steve Adams, recipient in 2013 of the prestigious Push Cart Award, for coming to the rescue when some of us wandered into the woods.

And last, but by no means least, a very special thanks to my mentor and friend, Amparo Garcia-Crow, whose thoughtful, steady guidance through this project and many others has been of immeasurable help. For keeping my feet on the ground and never losing sight of the goal posts, thank you, Ampy.

Aralyn Hughes, Editor

Cover artwork by Aralyn Hughes

It Happened in the '60s series by Jane Burkett

Book design by Mary-Ellen Campbell

Visit us at www.childfreewomen.com

We want your story. Please submit it for consideration on our website to http://childfree-women.com/contact-us/.

Made in the USA
Charleston, SC
21 March 2014